BODY
Athletic in appearance, ribs well sprung, chest deep and rather broad, loins deep and muscular, but not tucked up. Body slightly longer than height at shoulder.

SIZE
Ideal height for dogs 53 cms (21 ins); bitches slightly less.

HINDQUARTERS
Broad, muscular, in profile, sloping gracefully to set on of tail. Thighs long, deep and muscular with well turned stifles and strong well let down hocks. From hock to ground, hindlegs well boned and parallel when viewed from the rear.

TAIL
Moderately long, the bone reaching at least to hock, set on low, well furnished and with an upward swirl towards the end, completing graceful contour and balance of dog. Tail may be raised in excitement, never carried over the back.

FEET
Oval, pads deep, strong and sound, toes arched and close together. Nails short and strong.

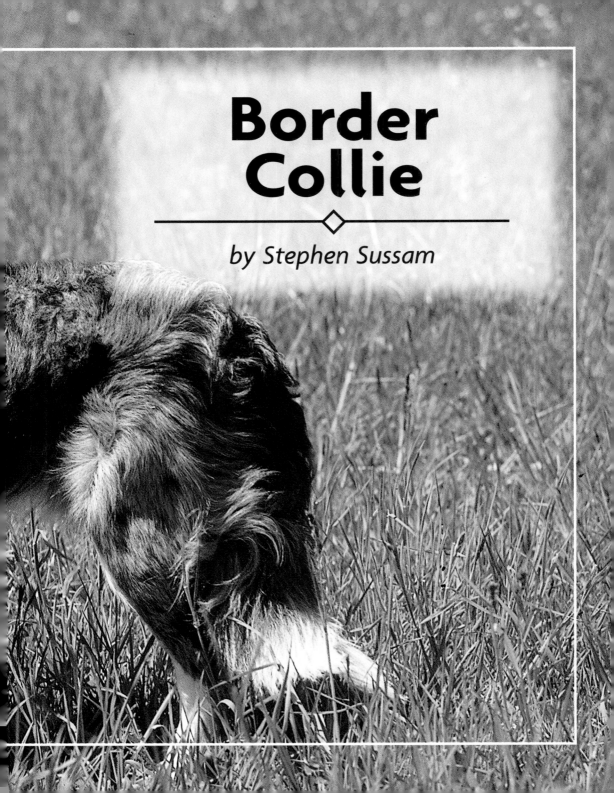

Border Collie

by Stephen Sussam

Table of Contents

DISTRIBUTED BY:

INTERPET
PUBLISHING
Vincent Lane, Dorking, Surrey RH4 3YX England

Copyright © 1999, **2006** • Kennel Club Books, LLC
Cover design patented: US 6,435,559 B2
Printed in South Korea
SECOND PRINTING

68

Photo Credits:

Norvia Behling
Carolina Biological Supply
Kent and Donna Dannen
Doskocil
Isabelle Francais
James Hayden-Yoav
James R Hayden, RBP
Carol Ann Johnson

Dwight R Kuhn
Dr Dennis Kunkel
Nancy Liguori
Mikki Pet Products
Phototake
Jean Claude Revy
Dr Andrew Spielman
C. James Webb

Illustrations by Renée Low

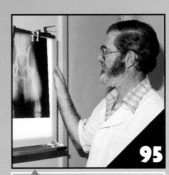

95

Housebreaking and Training Your Border Collie

by Charlotte Schwartz
Be informed about the importance of training your Border Collie, from the basics of housebreaking and understanding the development of a young dog to executing obedience commands (sit, stay, down, etc.).

123

Health Care of Your Border Collie

Discover how to select a proper veterinary surgeon and care for your dog at all stages of life. Topics include vaccination scheduling, skin problems, dealing with external and internal parasites and the medical conditions common to the breed.

Your Senior Border Collie

Recognise the signs of an ageing dog, both behavioural and medical; implement a senior-care programme with your veterinary surgeon and become comfortable with making the final decisions and arrangements for your senior Border Collie.

131

141

Showing Your Border Collie

Experience the dog show world, including different types of shows and the making up of a champion. Go beyond the conformation ring to working trials, gun dog trials, field and agility trials, etc.

Understanding the Behaviour of Your Border Collie

Learn to recognise and handle common behavioural problems in your Border Collie, including aggression with people and other dogs, chewing, barking, mounting, digging, jumping up, etc.

The Border Collie has been called the 'most intelligent dog in the world.' It can be a wonderful pet, guardian and loyal friend.

ORIGINS OF THE
Border Collie

Perhaps the Border Collie is not the most obvious choice of most pet owners given its great reputation as a working sheepdog. The breed's prowess in moving ornery flocks up and down hills is surely well known, as is its willingness to obey the shepherds. In our modern age, however, the Border Collie has gained new fame as 'the most intelligent dog in the world,' as certain popular dog books have acclaimed and the breed's accomplishments in the arenas of

obedience and agility trials attest. For the pet owner, this intelligence and willingness to obey translate into a tractable and loyal companion dog.

It is human nature rather than animal nature that becomes a consideration in this discussion of the Border Collie. We have all seen the individual who chooses to drive the sleekest racing machine along the common thoroughfare to work and back, or perhaps the person who purchases the all-terrain technological triumph, a vehicle ready for the Paris to Dakar Rally, for the trip to school or market. To so under-employ such technology or expertise must be a factor of imagination or conspicuous display. Or perhaps admiration.

Let us agree that it is admiration and the love of so perfect and honourable a breed that compels the new potential owner, who lives nowhere near a farm and whose business with sheep occurs only during sleepless nights, to purchase and share his life with a Border Collie. Given the breed's original purpose, owning a Border Collie as a pet is, in the strictest sense, incorrect. The history, purpose and heart of the animal itself converge upon one utilitarian theme: work. This is a working dog and those who choose it as a pet for whatever reasons of admiration, emulation or reverse snobbery must understand and accommodate its practical soul.

The ancient and necessary truce that first brought man and

The Border Collie has always been widely used in handling sheep. It was bred first and foremost as a working dog.

dog together is slightly outside our scope. The relevant point is that the working Border Collie evolved from early guarding and herding animals. Most writers call upon the 1570 *Treatise of Englishe Dogges* by John Caius as the first printed reference to the working sheepdog:

The essential characteristics of the Border Collie have not changed over hundreds of years.

'This dogge, either at the hearing of his master's voyce, or at the wagging and whisteling in his fist, or at his shrill and hoarse hissing bringeth the wandering weathers and straying sheepe into the self same place where his master's will and wishe is to have them, whereby the shepherd reapeth this benefite, namely, that with little labour and no toyle or moving of his feete he may rule and guide his flocke, according to his owne desire, either to have them go forward, or to stand still, or to drawe backward, or to turne this way to take that way. For it is not in Englande as it is in Fraunce, as it is in Flaunders, as it is in Syria, as it is in Tartaria, where the sheepe follow the shepherd, for heere in our country, the shepherd followeth the sheepe. And sometimes the straying sheepe, when no dogge runneth before them, gather themselves together in a flocke when they hear the shepherd whistel in his fist, for feare of the dogge (as I imagine) remembering this (if unreasonable creatures may be reported to have memory) that the dogge commonly runneth out at his master's warrant which is his whistel. This have we often times diligently marcked in taking our journey from towne to towne. When we have heard a shepherd whistel, we have rayned in our horse and stood styll a space to see the proofe and trial of this matter. Furthermore with this dogge doth the shepherd take the sheepe for ye slaughter and to be healed if they be sicke, no hurt or harme in the world done to the simple creature.'

Although the appearance of the dog is not described here, the performance is that of the modern Border Collie. The essence of that performance has not changed for hundreds of years, and in regard to sheep herding, neither has the Border Collie. Skills have been refined and perfected as prized workers were selectively bred and sold. Appearance, although never a true concern of breeders and owners of this animal, changed little since 1790 when a woodcut in *Bewick's History of Quadrapeds* depicted a shepherd's dog that bears a resounding resemblance to today's Border Collie.

Of course, a shepherd's dog, a sheepdog, is any dog that works with sheep and not necessarily a 'collie.' Although the origin and exact meaning of the name remains unknown, some contend that it comes from the word *coley*, denoting black; others say it comes from the Welsh word *coelius*, meaning faithful; whilst

The Rough Collie, sometimes called the Scotch Collie, is closely related to the Border Collie. It is a more substantial dog with an abundant double coat.

A SCOTTISH 'TWEED'

The winner of the very first sheepdog trial was a sheepdog from Scotland by the name of Tweed. He was owned by Jaime Thomson and won the event at Bala in North Wales in 1873. The entry fee was an astounding £10, a grand sum in 1873.

still others claim that the name comes from *colley*, referring to a Scottish type of sheep. The designation 'Border' is easier to trace, describing the area where the dogs were prominently used, the Welsh and Scottish borders of England.

The modern Collie has been divided into five separate breeds: the Rough Collie, the Smooth Collie, the Shetland Sheepdog, the Bearded Collie and the Border Collie. The popularity of these breeds with the general public began with the favour bestowed

KING OF THE HILL

Whilst many farmers have attempted to replace their dogs with mechanical devices, most have failed miserably! As any shepherd will confirm, a good Border Collie is worth his weight in Crown Jewels! The Collies that work in the hill country have the most difficult of tasks and terrain. Neither tractors nor motor bikes can manoeuvre over rocks, hills and streams, where the Border Collie is called upon to cast out the hill sheep, which are about as light and agile as the Collie himself.

11

The English Shepherd is an American spin-off of the Border Collie. Not widely known in its homeland, the English Shepherd is primarily a stock dog.

BEYOND THE SHEEP AND COWS

The Border Collie has been offered employment on a variety of livestock beyond the usual ovine and bovine types. Reports of Border Collies as poultry pushers, working successfully with geese, chickens, turkeys and ducks, have stirred 'down' many feathers. Some Collies have even ruffled the ostrich's feathers. Of the four-legged varieties, the Border Collie has stared down the likes of buffalo, emu, goats, pigs, alpaca, rhea, fallows and sitka deer. Given the breed's talents, this roster could one day be as lengthy as Noah's!

upon them by Queen Victoria, who owned several. An 1860 portrait of one of her dogs, Gypsie, shows us a mostly black animal who today would be taken for a purebred Border Collie. Although the predominant portraiture displays a Rough Collie, it can be inferred that the Border Collie was the original type from which the more elegant breeds were developed. These Rough Collies were bred taller, with more emphasis upon a full coat, longer, narrower heads and refined colour. In addition, there are many other types of herding dogs in the world bred from Border Collie stock, including the Australian Kelpie and the American cousins: the Australian Shepherd, the Farm Collie, the English Shepherd and the McNab. The histories of these

The Australian Shepherd is American, not Australian, despite its name. Approximately the same size as the Border Collie, the Aussie is squarer, heavier coated and slightly taller.

colonial relatives are as similar to the British Border Collie as are their looks and characteristics. All are working stock dogs and were imported to these countries during the last century along with the Scots and the sheep who began the vast sheep ranches. Many of these working

NIPPING THE BOVINE

Barking and baying at sleeping cows is no pastime for the quick-minded Border Collie. Whilst many of the traditional cattle dogs, such as the Bouvier des Flandres and the Australian Cattle Dog, stir their cows by barking, the Border Collie is a quiet worker that moves the cows by nipping at their feet. The cows often try to kick the dogs, but the Collie's low stance keeps them out of hooves' way.

The scantily clad brother of the Rough Collie, the Smooth Collie is far less popular in the UK though it is equally talented and intelligent.

animals are not registered because their ancestors arrived before there was a registry in England.

The Border Collie, not moulded to a particular physical standard, continued to be bred for work and work alone. While modern Border Collies can all be traced to a few distinguished forebears, other breeds have been introduced from time to time with the aim of improving working performance. In fact, the most famous characteristic of the Border Collie, the power of the

eye to control stock, was bred into the breed from gundogs like setters, pointers and spaniels. James Hogg, the Scottish shepherd poet, wrote in 1790 a description of a dog showing 'eye' which is applicable to any Border Collie today:

'Whenever the dog was within doors, his whole occupation was watching and pointing the cat from morning to night. When she flitted from one place to another, so did he in a moment; and then squatting down, he kept his point sedulously till he was either called off or fell asleep.'

A related result of this early

The Australian Cattle Dog, more vocal than the Border Collie, is often compared to the Border Collie for its intelligence and natural working ability.

13

The Shetland Sheepdog, a close relation of the Border Collie, is a miniature version of the Rough Collie. He stands only two-thirds the height of the Border Collie.

crossbreeding with gundogs is well-developed scenting ability and the retrieving instincts of Border Collies. These abilities are made good use of in obedience trials but are sometimes a problem for dogs that are tempted away from work at the scent of a rabbit.

The International Sheep Dog Society (ISDS) was created in 1906. These early owners and handlers set out to protect and improve the breed through working trials and a registry. A stud book was first compiled in 1951, listing over 14,000 dogs. The book has grown by over 6,000 registrations each

The Border Collie's farm work necessitates that he be able to work with all types of animals.

SEE AMERICA'S FIVE!
Although the United States has originated very few of its own breeds of dog (compared to Great Britain), breeders there have yielded five interesting sheepdogs, all cousins to our Border Collie. The only breed to be fully recognised by the American Kennel Club is our 'first cousin,' the Australian Shepherd. The Aussie, as he is often called, standing 18 to 23 inches, is a handsome symmetrical tailless stock dog with an elegant medium-length coat. The English Shepherd is a stockier, squarer dog than the Border Collie, from which it derives. These lesser known sheepdogs developed in the Midwest and East and are nearly identical to the Farm Collie. The Farm Collies are merely crosses of Border Collies imported into the U.S. used for various type of farm and ranch work. The McNab, named for its importer Alexander McNab of California, is a medium-built dog with a smooth coat and prick ears. Like the Border Collie, it is usually black and white. The Basque Shepherd is a direct descendant of the Australian Shepherd, appearing identical except that he maintains his tail! Unlike his tailless brother, he is not recognised by the AKC.

year since then. A common entry in the stud book would show the influence of the bloodlines created by J. M. Wilson, the most renowned Border Collie breeder and handler of all time. His

Breeding Border Collies strictly for the show ring often compromises their working abilities.

Whitehope dogs are the basis of many modern pedigrees. Today the Border Collie is also recognised in the show ring, and whilst there is insistence that the animal not be bred away from its working ability, the close breeding favoured by those who breed to show can often result in undesirable characteristics being passed on by the attractive but untested non-working dogs.

A COLLIE BY ANY OTHER COLOUR...

In England and Ireland, the Border Collie is a black and white affair. In the U.S., however, where the diversity

of the 'Rainbow' reigns, other colours are beginning to become commonplace. The once rare chocolate or liver has become popular. Other colours that can be spotted on Border Collies include: silver (black with white speckling), blue merle, slate grey (or blue), sable, lemon (yellow), ginger (red), fawn (a dilute liver) and brindle (combination of brown and black). Let's not forget that solid white Border Collies are not frowned upon in the U.S. as they are in the U.K.

THE EYES HAVE IT!

Border Collies possess a unique working trait in their ability to move stock with just their eyes. This ability to 'stare down' the sheep in order to move them is called 'strong eye' and is believed to be inherited from crosses to gundogs years ago. Whilst some herding dogs bark, circle and nip to move their woolly charges, the Border Collie merely uses its unswerving stare to move the flock along.

CHARACTERISTICS OF THE
Border Collie

A Border Collie's work is not limited to sheep; they often work with cattle as well.

The Border Collie's character as outlined by its description is entirely related to the breed's occupation and purpose. While this holds special relevance to the owner of working Border Collies, the pet owner should appreciate these long-developed, characteristic essentials of the working specimen and will see evidence of these instincts in his pet. In many cases it would require specific training to fully revive and solidify these instincts, but understanding the dog's background gives the pet owner insight into his Border Collie's behaviour, personality and natural aptitudes. The unique terms that are used in defining the Border Collie's traits, clear to the farmer or shepherd, need further explanation to the pet owner.

THE BORDER COLLIE DEFINED
OUTRUN

The Border Collie must not simply chase sheep but be able to turn and direct them. The dog does not travel in straight lines, but runs out wide to gather the sheep. The dog who lacks an instinctual cast, or turning ability, will cut in too close to the sheep, merely startling them, not gathering them. A dog with a good outrun will naturally know how to keep the proper distance between himself and the sheep.

DID YOU KNOW?

The inborn qualities of a top Border Collie must include:

• A natural cast or outrun
• Sufficient eye to gather and control sheep
• Power enough to face down and direct a single sheep without rushing or biting
• Intelligence, which allows him to take the initiative when necessary
• Temperament equal to training and occasional correction without sulking, snarling or running away
• A strong constitution

'Eye' is a unique quality of the Border Collie. This dog approaches the sheep with the characteristic stare and his head held low.

EYE

Eye is one of the most unique qualities of the Border Collie and the most interesting instinct that you may observe in your pet. It is an attribute that has taken many generations to breed into the animal. Eye is a mesmerizing gaze that the dog levels at sheep, holding them in position. The Border Collie's stance is rigid, with the body and head held low, roughly similar to a gundog as it points. This ability, in fact, may have been added to the Border Collie from breeding with hunters. Strong-eyed dogs can hold a bunch of sheep in the open with little running about.

POWER

Power is the rather undefinable ability of the top dog to dominate and assert mastery over sheep without aggressive barking or biting. A dog with power holds

DID YOU KNOW?

The usual and rightful occupation for the Border Collie is farm work. Here, these silent working and strong-eyed dogs are employed in several categories of work, which may be described as:
• work with sheep on hills
• work with lowland sheep
• work with dairy cows
• work with dry cattle
• work with rough cattle (drovers and dealers' dogs)
• work loading and penning sheep
• work in yards (shearers', dealers' and contractors' dogs)

No single dog is capable of this variety of performance. Training and environment therefore further divide the Border Collie into categories of hill dog, lowland sheepdog, cow dog, cattle dog, rough cattle dog and sheep dealer's dog.

authority over his flock without terrifying or spooking the sheep.

INTELLIGENCE

Intelligence in the Border Collie cannot be likened to humanness. It is so closely bound with working instinct and the desire to please that it may not be describ-

The strongest instinct bred into the Border Collie is the desire to work.

able out of this context. In the working dog, intelligence is not inventive but innately correct when confronted with any decision involving the task for which it is bred. It is wonderfully clear but humanly puzzling in its adherence to a functional and practical hierarchy. Consider its allegiance to its master, so unyielding that a bitch will allow that person to take her puppies away, even drown them, without anger or objection.

TEMPERAMENT

The strongest desire bred into the Border Collie is the desire to work. This is the result of centuries of development and dominates even the survival instinct in some collies. These dogs can become frustrated and destructive if they find themselves in an environment with nothing

for them to do. A dog of this sort does not always make a good pet and yet the careful and considerate owner can surmount this instinctual difficulty by making his Border Collie a functional and important part of the family. Guarding his human family and their property is also demanding work. The important thing is to keep your dog interested, occupied and active. The farm, after all, has probably more 'down time' built into its schedule than the average, on-the-go, weather-impervious, modern suburban family.

Dedication to work, which is obviously not a fault in the working dog, can result in neurotic pet dogs and is the consequence of breeding for performance rather than temperament. Nervousness, in general, is the most common personality problem in the Border Collie. There is, of course, only a fine line between the sensitively tuned working animal and one that exhibits nervousness. The distinction is related to environment and occupation.

The fact that obedience is such a strong instinct makes training the Border Collie a truly rewarding enterprise. No dog learns faster and retains what he has learned longer. Remember, however, that because your Border Collie is so eager to perform and please, and consequently so

WHAT'S IN A NAME?

There is more that goes into naming a Border Collie than meets the eye. While for a pet dog any name that you fancy is fine, there is a convention in the naming of working dogs. A working dog requires a short name that is simple to pronounce and will be unmistakably heard in the long-range, abrupt and often complicated communications of the farmer or shepherd. Classic and popular names for males have been Ben, Lad, Roy and Cap; favourites for bitches have included Nell, Meg and Jess.

should be socialised early and handled by all members of the family in order to avoid this condition.

It is especially worthwhile to note the importance of exercise as relates to your Border Collie's mental (and, of course, physical) well-being. Do not think that a daily walk on a lead will provide your Border Collie with enough exercise. You must find a secure open area (such as your fenced-in garden) in which your dog can run free for a period of time. Anything short of this may produce a neurotic, unhappy animal. As for outside housing, do not be surprised if you find your pet more often on the roof of his

Border Collie are success–oriented and driven to please.

house than inside it.

Boredom and frustrated herding instincts may cause your dog to engage in a very dangerous behaviour that, unfortunately, is rather common in pet Border Collies: car chasing. The combination of the instinctive 'eye' and 'outrun' with the lure of cars and local traffic is the leading cause of accidental death among pets of this breed. Sufficient activity and training will diminish this hazard but will never entirely eliminate

disappointed at failure, your training should be gentle whilst being firm. Rough bullying methods may seem to get obedience, but obedience without trust will soon be forgotten.

Shyness and sulkiness are other faults of temperament sometimes found in the Border Collie that may interfere with training. Again these faults are related to the dog's deep desire to perform; these dogs cannot bear to fail or disappoint their masters. Training such dogs is difficult since they will not stand any correction, even the gentlest reproof.

The Border Collie can sometimes be a one-person animal, so attuned to his master that others may fail to elicit his attention or obedience. Pet dogs

19

it. Even when your Border Collie is completely and safely trained, it is still necessary to keep him on lead in open areas and to only let him off lead in enclosed areas.

APPEARANCE

There are wide variations in the appearance of the Border Collie. This is the result of the attitude that the ability to work is far more important than the looks of the animal. The modern breed standard takes into account the practical nature of the animal and therefore allows exceptional variety in colour, size and coat whilst demanding one thing above all—-soundness.

As long as appearance does

not come to dominate the breeding and perception of the dog, there is certainly room in our admiration for the Border Collie to discuss, and even to idealize, some aspects of appearance.

The head shape should reveal at a glance the gender of the collie. The classic type is wedge shaped, but smaller foxy types are often seen, as are pointer types with domed skulls. The ears may stand up, bend over or lie flat. Eyes should generally be brown, although blue eyes are quite common.

Conformation is extremely important because of its link to performance. The dog works with its head low, and a long neck is

A NOTE ABOUT HEALTH...

The most serious hereditary defect in the Border Collie is progressive retinal atrophy (PRA), also known as 'night blindness.' Because this disease is controlled by a recessive gene, it is hard to eradicate in the breed. Its diagnosis is often uncertain because of its progressive nature. Some dogs never go completely blind, while others are blind by three or four years of age. Collie eye anomaly (CEA), a blinding condition prevalent in the Rough Collie, is relatively uncommon in the Border Collie.

Hip dysplasia is seen in the Border Collie, although it is not often readily evident in non-working dogs.

A Border Collie nips the heels of the horse from a crouched position so that the horse cannot kick him.

ideal. The smooth-coated dog is best in both the practical and the aesthetic sense. Border Collies can also be found with coats as fine as those of greyhounds, but obviously these are not adequately protected from the vicissitudes of rough working conditions.

Many of the Border Collies registered today are black-and-white in colour. The distribution of colour can follow any pattern but black dominance is preferred. Tri-colours (black, white and tan) are common. Variations of brown colouring, from russet to liver, are seen, as are greys and blue and red merles. While all colours and patterns are accepted, white markings have a utilitarian value because they help the farmer locate the dog in the field.

necessary for balance. Shoulders should be well laid back to facilitate speed and reduce jarring on sudden stops. Long legs and a broad chest mean more speed and plenty of lung and heart room. Length in the back and hips is necessary for stamina and grace. The tail should be carried low.

Preference for coat type is also dictated by practicality. Dogs with woolly coats are at a disadvantage in the field and in bad weather. Stickers, burrs, mud and snow will collect on his belly and legs and between his pads. Such coats will invite fleas, encourage skin problems and engender a terrible smell when wet. Straight, silky hair with a dense undercoat is

NATURAL APTITUDES AND ACTIVITIES

The Border Collie's instinctual abilities have been adapted to many activities other than herding and farming. One very well-known activity is the sheepdog trial. While not exclusively a showcase for Border Collies, trials seem to be dominated by the breed. Sheepdog trials first began in 1873 as a way, when all is considered, to show off the hard-earned skills of a farmer's dog and to prove one's dog better than another's. Today the aim promoted by the International Sheep Dog Society is to improve the breed of

Border Collies work hard, but they also need to rest in order to conserve their energies for work.

sheepdogs for herding by encouraging competition. The trials are based on farm work or, more correctly, on the type of work done by a sheepdog on a hilly farm. They basically test the skills of outrun, lift, drive, pen and shed. The handler sends his dog from 200 to 400 yards to fetch a small number of sheep, usually four or five. The dog must run well out in order not to send the sheep back into the pens. The dog must then bring the sheep through a gate, steer them around the handler, drive them away and through another gate, turn them and drive them across the course, negotiate a third set of gates and

then drive the sheep back to a gated pen. After this, the dog must send the sheep out of the pen and drive them off the course.

Obedience and agility are also two areas in which the Border Collie excels. Competition of both types are dominated by the breed. These trials celebrate the instinctive obedience and natural agility of the Border Collie. If you have ever observed one of these trials, you cannot help but notice that Border Collies are present in droves…and they consistently finish well. The relationship of these tests to the actual work for which the Border Collie was intended is marginal, but they

Training a Border Collie can be quite a rewarding endeavour. Intelligence, trainability and willingness to please make the Border Collie very popular as a pet and companion.

offer a welcome outlet for the pet dog's energy as well as training goals for dog and owner.

Border Collies are sometimes used as guide dogs for the blind, but more often the collies used for this job are crossbred with either Labrador or Golden Retrievers. Purebred Border Collies are generally too quick and sudden in their movements for this occupation. Their hardiness and persistence, however, make them excellent choices for Mountain Rescue animals. Bitches, with short coats that resist snow and mud, are preferred here. Borders used for this purpose should be relatively friendly and loose eyed; that is, with less of the instinctual tendency to stop and level the mesmerising stare known as 'eye.'

GOOD OWNER, GOOD PET

As often stated, the Border Collie is primarily a working dog, but this is not exclusively so. Its intelligence lends it a quality of adaptability that, given the right owner, may make pet life nearly as satisfying for the dog as the working career for which it was born and bred. So in the end, we come back to our beginning consideration—human nature. Can the pet owner understand the needs of his Border Collie and mediate between the animal's instincts and its environment? If so, then this expertly engineered working dog can become an enjoyable pet. As with any breed, all other considerations aside, it is good owners who make good pets.

The face-off. Border Collies are experts at mesmerising other animals with their stares.

BREED STANDARD FOR THE
Border Collie

While not the 'main stage' of the Border Collie's auspicious talents, dog shows are another arena in which the breed's qualities are displayed. The conformation show is considered by some breed experts to present a danger to the carefully bred instincts of the Border Collie. The enthusiasm for dog shows has caused other working breeds to come mere caricatures of their former utilitarian selves. The International Sheep Dog Society, which registers over 6,000 Border Collies each year, and The Kennel Club, which accepted the breed in 1976 and granted it Championship status in 1986, understand this concern. In order to qualify for the title of Champion, a Border Collie must not only win in the show ring but also prove that it can work sheep. Sheepdogs that rank in Open Sheep Trials or qualify for the National or International Sheep Dog Trials are exempted from this working test.

A breed standard, which is a written description of an ideal representative of a breed, is used by judges and breeders to determine the relative merits and faults of a dog. By definition, such a standard must describe each

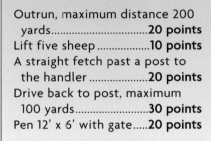

DID YOU KNOW?

A Border Collie must score at least 60 points within a time limit of 15 minutes to pass a working test, which must be passed in order for the Border Collie to become a Champion. The test consists of the following tasks and point schedule:

Outrun, maximum distance 200 yards.................................**20 points**
Lift five sheep.................**10 points**
A straight fetch past a post to the handler ....**20 points**
Drive back to post, maximum 100 yards.......................**30 points**
Pen 12' x 6' with gate.....**20 points**

_____

TOTAL.............................**100 points**

part of the dog, keeping in mind the working attributes that make each physical attribute advantageous to the dog. The breed standard of The Kennel Club for the Border Collie strives to keep the breed's working characteristics in view. Whether this attitude will remain and prevail is the responsibility of every true lover of the breed. Whilst the Border Collie varies significantly in many working lines, where conformation is far less important than performance, breeders still attempt to balance the equation by producing handsome, harmonious dogs with outstanding working ability.

THE KENNEL CLUB STANDARD FOR THE BORDER COLLIE

General Appearance: Well proportioned, smooth outline showing quality, gracefulness, and perfect balance, combined with sufficient substance to give the impression of endurance. Any tendency to coarseness or weediness is undesirable.

Characteristics: Tenacious, hard working sheep dog, of great tractability.

Temperament: Keen, alert, responsive and intelligent. Neither nervous nor aggressive.

Head and Skull: Skull fairly broad, occiput not pronounced. Cheeks not full or rounded. Muzzle, tapering to nose, moderately short and strong. Skull and foreface approximately equal in length. Stop very distinct. Nose black, except in brown or chocolate colour when it may be brown. In blues, nose should be slate colour. Nostrils well developed.

Eyes: Set wide apart, oval shaped, of moderate size, brown in colour except in merles where one or both or part of one or both may be blue. Expression mild, keen, alert and intelligent.

Ears: Medium size and texture, set well apart. Carried erect or semi-erect and sensitive in use.

Mouth: Teeth and jaws strong with perfect, regular and complete scissor bite, i.e., upper teeth closely overlapping lower teeth and set square to jaw.

Neck: Of good length, strong and muscular, slightly arched and broadening to the shoulders.

Forequarters: Front legs parallel when viewed from the front, pasterns slightly sloping when viewed from side. Bone strong but not heavy. Shoulders well laid back, elbows close to body.

Body: Athletic in appearance, ribs well sprung, chest deep and rather broad, loins deep and muscular, but not tucked up. Body slightly longer than height at shoulder.

Hindquarters: Broad, muscular, in profile sloping gracefully to set on of tail. Thighs long, deep and muscular with well turned stifles and strong well let down hocks. From hock to ground, hindlegs well boned and parallel when viewed from rear.

HEAD

Muzzle tapers to nose, distinct stop, skull and foreface should be approximately equal in length.

BODY

Athletic in appearance; body should be slightly longer than height at shoulder (left), not square (right).

EARS

Medium size and set well apart (left), not too large and close together (right).

CHEST

Chest and loins should be deep and muscular (left), not tucked up (right).

TAIL

Moderately long and low set, with upward swirl at end (left), never carried over back (right).

Feet: Oval, pads deep, strong and sound, toes arched and close together. Nails short and strong.

Tail: Moderately long, the bone reaching at least to hock, set on low, well furnished and with an upward swirl towards the end, completing graceful contour and balance of dog. Tail may be raised in excitement, never carried over back.

Gait/Movement: Free, smooth and tireless, with minimum lift of feet, conveying impression of ability to move with great stealth and speed.

Coat: Two varieties:
1) Moderately long; 2) Smooth.

In both, topcoat dense and medium textured, undercoat soft and dense giving good weather resistance. In moderately long-coated variety, abundant coat forms mane, breeching and brush. On face, ears, forelegs (except for feather), hindlegs from hock to ground, hair should be short and smooth.

Colour: Variety of colours permissible. White should never predominate.

Size: Ideal height: dogs 53 cms (21 ins); bitches slightly less.

Faults: Any departure from the foregoing points should be considered a fault and the seriousness with which the fault should be regarded should be in exact proportion to its degree.

Note: Male animals should have two apparently normal testicles fully descended into the scrotum.

A wide variety of colours and patterns are acceptable for the Border Collie. A partially white dog is acceptable, but white should not be the dominant colour.

Border Collie

WHERE TO BEGIN?
If you are convinced that the Border Collie is the ideal dog for you, it's time to learn about where to find a puppy and what to look for. Locating a litter of Border Collies should not present a problem for the new owner. You should inquire about breeders in your area who enjoy a good reputation in the breed. You are looking for an established breeder with outstanding dog ethics and a strong commitment to the breed. New owners should have as many questions as they have doubts. An established breeder is indeed the one to answer your four million questions and make you comfortable with your choice of the Border Collie. An established breeder will sell you a puppy at a fair price if, and only if, the breeder determines that you are a suitable, worthy owner of his/her dogs. An established breeder can be relied upon for advice, no matter what time of day or night. A reputable breeder will accept a puppy back, without questions, should you decide that this is not the right dog for you.

When choosing a breeder, reputation is much more important than convenience of location. Do not be overly impressed by breeders who run brag advertisements in the presses about their stupendous champions and working lines. The real quality breeders are quiet and unassuming. You hear about them at the dog trials and shows, by word of mouth. You may be well advised to avoid the novice who lives only a couple miles away. The local novice breeder, trying so hard to get rid of that first litter of puppies, is more than accommodating and

DID YOU KNOW?
Your selection of a good puppy can be determined by your needs. A show potential or a good pet? It is your choice. Every puppy, however, should be of good temperament. Although show-quality puppies are bred and raised with emphasis on physical conformation, responsible breeders strive for equally good temperament. Do not buy from a breeder who concentrates solely on physical beauty at the expense of personality.

anxious to sell you one. That breeder will charge you as much as any established breeder. The novice breeder isn't going to interrogate you and your family about your intentions with the puppy, the environment and training you can provide, etc. That breeder will be nowhere to be found when your poorly bred, badly adjusted four-pawed monster starts to growl and spit up at midnight or eat the family cat!

Whilst health considerations in the Border Collie are not nearly as daunting as in most other breeds, socialisation is a breeder concern of immense importance. Since the Border Collie's temperament can vary from line to line, socialisation is the first and best way to encourage a proper, stable personality.

Choosing a breeder is an important first step in dog ownership. Fortunately, the

majority of Border Collie breeders are devoted to the breed and its well being. New owners should have little problem finding a reputable breeder who doesn't live on the other side of the country (or in a different country). The Kennel Club is able to recommend breeders of quality Border Collies, as can any local all-breed club or Border Collie club.

DID YOU KNOW?

If the breeder from whom you are buying a puppy asks you a lot of personal questions, do not be insulted. Such a breeder wants to be sure that you will be a fit provider for his puppy.

Potential owners are encouraged to attend sheepdog trials to see the Border Collies in action, to meet the farmers and handlers firsthand and to get an idea what Border Collies look like outside of a photographer's lens. Provided you approach the handlers when they are not terribly busy with the dogs, most are more than willing to answer questions, recommend breeders and give advice.

Now that you have contacted and met a breeder or two and made your choice about which breeder is best suited to your needs, it's time to visit the

DID YOU KNOW?

Breeders rarely release puppies until they are eight to ten weeks of age. This is an acceptable age for most breeds of dog, excepting toy breeds which are not released until around 12 weeks, given their petite sizes. If a breeder has a puppy that is 12 weeks or more, it is likely well socialised and housetrained. Be sure that it is otherwise healthy before deciding to take it home.

Collies generally have small litters, averaging five puppies, so selection is limited once you have located a desirable litter. While the basic structure of the breed has little variation, the temperament may present trouble in certain strains. Beware of the shy or overly aggressive puppy: be especially conscious of the nervous Border Collie pup. Do not let sentiment or emotion trap you into buying the runt of the litter.

If you have intentions of your new charge herding sheep, there are many more considerations. The parents of a future working dog should have excellent qualifications, including actual work experience as well as working titles in their pedigrees.

The gender of your puppy is largely a matter of personal taste, although there is a common belief amongst those

Your breeder can help evaluate your Border Collie pup's conformation if you plan to show your dog.

litter. Keep in mind that many top breeders have waiting lists. Sometimes new owners have to wait as long as two years for a puppy. If you are really committed to the breeder whom you've selected, then you will wait (and hope for an early arrival!). If not, you may have to resort to your second or third choice breeder. Don't be too anxious, however. If the breeder doesn't have any waiting list, or any customers, there is probably a good reason. It's no different than visiting a pub with no clientele. The better pubs and restaurants always have a waiting list—and it is usually worth the wait. Besides, isn't a puppy more important than a pint?

Since you are likely choosing a Border Collie as a pet dog and not a working dog, you simply should select a pup that is friendly and attractive. Border

DID YOU KNOW?

Your puppy should have a well-fed appearance but not a distended abdomen, which may indicate worms or incorrect feeding, or both. The body should be firm, with a solid feel. The skin of the abdomen should be pale pink and clean, without signs of scratching or rash. Check the hind legs to make certain that dewclaws were removed, if any were present at birth.

who work with Border Collies that bitches are quicker to learn and generally more loving and faithful. Males learn more slowly but retain the lesson longer. The difference in size is noticeable but slight. Colouration is not a grave concern with this breed, although there have been countless treatises upon the desirable amount of white and

DID YOU KNOW?

If you lead an erratic, unpredictable life, with daily or weekly changes in your work requirements, consider the problems of owning a puppy. The new puppy has to be fed regularly, socialised (loved, petted, handled, introduced to other people) and, most importantly, allowed to visit outdoors for toilet training. As the dog gets older, it can be more tolerant of deviations in its feeding and toilet relief.

black on sheepdogs. Some theories claim that too much black on a Collie will frighten the sheep, who only accept white animals in their flocks. This might seem like good sense or balderdash, depending on your family's feelings about its black sheep! Nevertheless, a good stable dog, with working abilities, can be any colour and owners should curb their preconceived notions about the

colour of their Collies.

Because litters are small and because Border Collies are primarily workers rather than pets, commercial breeders are less attracted to the breed. This also helps your selection, ensuring that most pups will come from strong working lines unencumbered by overbreeding, inbreeding or the countless finicky prejudices that have damaged other breeds. Prices will generally be lower than that of other breeds but higher in city areas where a percentage of the dogs will be sold for pets or show dogs. Look in farming newspapers and journals to find the best Border Collies.

Breeders commonly allow visitors to see the litter by around the fifth or sixth week, and puppies leave for their new homes between the eighth and tenth week. Breeders who permit their puppies to leave early are more interested in your pounds than their puppies' well being. Puppies need to learn the rules of the trade from their dams, and most dams continue teaching the pups manners and dos and don'ts until around the eighth week. Breeders spend significant amounts of time with the Border Collie toddlers so that they are able to interact with the 'other species', i.e., humans. Given the long history that dogs and humans have,

'Take us home, please!' When you meet the Border Collie pup for you, you will know it!

bonding between the two species is natural but must be nurtured. A well-bred, well-socialised Border Collie pup wants nothing more than to be near you and please you.

Always check the bite of your selected puppy to be sure that it is neither overshot nor undershot. This may not be too noticeable on a young puppy

DID YOU KNOW?

An important consideration to be discussed is the sex of your puppy. For a family companion, a bitch may be the better choice, considering the female's inbred concern for all young creatures and her accompanying tolerance and patience. It is always advised to spay a pet bitch, which may guarantee her a longer life.

Puppy teeth can be misleading... although small, they are very sharp and capable of inflicting pain.

but it is a fairly common problem with certain lines of Border Collies.

COMMITMENT OF OWNERSHIP

After considering all of these factors, you have most likely already made some very important decisions about selecting your puppy. You have

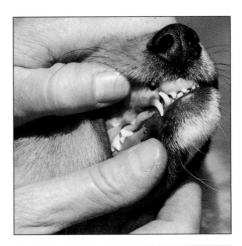

As a young Border Collie loses his puppy teeth, they are replaced with strong adult teeth. This Border Collie has a clean, healthy smile.

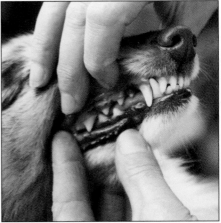

The standard calls for a perfect scissors bite with the upper teeth closely overlapping the lower teeth.

DID YOU KNOW?

Two important documents you will get from the breeder are the pup's pedigree and registration papers. The breeder should register the litter and each pup with The Kennel Club, and it is necessary for you to have the paperwork if you plan on showing or breeding in the future.

Make sure you know the breeder's intentions on which type of registration he will obtain for the pup. There are limited registrations which may prohibit the dog from being shown or from competing in non-conformation trials such as Working or Agility if the breeder feels that the pup is not of sufficient quality to do so. There is also a type of registration that will permit the dog in non-conformation competition only.

If your dog is registered with a Kennel-Club-recognised breed club, then you can register the pup with The Kennel Club yourself. Your breeder can assist you with the specifics of the registration process.

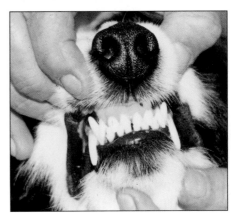

individual personality—perhaps you have even found one that particularly appeals to you.

However, even if you have not yet found the Border Collie puppy of your dreams, observing pups will help you learn to recognise certain behaviour and to determine what a pup's behaviour indicates about his temperament. You will be able to pick out which pups are the leaders, which ones are less

Border Collies become completely dedicated to their owners. Be sure YOU are ready to reciprocate this love and devotion, as your pet Border Collie depends on you for proper care.

chosen a Border Collie, which means that you have decided which characteristics you want in a dog and what type of dog will best fit into your family and lifestyle. If you have selected a breeder, you have gone a step further—you have done your research and found a responsible, conscientious person who breeds quality Border Collies and who should be a reliable source of help as you and your puppy adjust to life together. If you have observed a litter in action, you have obtained a firsthand look at the dynamics of a puppy 'pack' and, thus, you should learn about each pup's

DID YOU KNOW?

Unfortunately, when a puppy is bought by someone who does not take into consideration the time and attention that dog ownership requires, it is the puppy who suffers when he is either abandoned or placed in a shelter by a frustrated owner. So all of the 'homework' you do in preparation for your pup's arrival will benefit you both. The more informed you are, the more you will know what to expect and the better equipped you will be to handle the ups and downs of raising a puppy. Hopefully, everyone in the household is willing to do his part in raising and caring for the pup. The anticipation of owning a dog often brings a lot of promises from excited family members: 'I will walk him every day,' 'I will feed him,' 'I will housebreak him,' etc., but these things take time and effort, and promises can easily be forgotten once the novelty of the new pet has worn off.

outgoing, which ones are confident, which ones are shy, playful, friendly, aggressive, etc. Equally as important, you will learn to recognise what a healthy pup should look and act like. All of these things will help you in your search, and when you find the Border Collie that was meant for you, you will know it!

DID YOU KNOW?

Many good breeders will offer you insurance with your new puppy, which is an excellent idea. The first few weeks of insurance will probably be covered free of charge or with only minimal cost, allowing you to take up the policy when this expires. If you own a pet dog, it is sensible to take out such a policy as veterinary fees can be high, although routine vaccinations and boosters are not covered. Look carefully at the many options open to you before deciding which suits you best.

Researching your breed, selecting a responsible breeder and observing as many pups as possible are all important steps on the way to dog ownership. It may seem like a lot of effort...and you have not even brought the pup home yet! Remember, though, you cannot be too careful when it comes to deciding on the type of dog you

want and finding out about your prospective pup's background. Buying a puppy is not—or should not be—just another whimsical purchase. This is one instance in which you actually do get to choose your own family! You may be thinking that buying a puppy should be fun—it should not be so serious and so much work. Keep in mind that your puppy is not a cuddly stuffed toy or decorative lawn ornament, but a creature that will become a real member of your family. You will come to realise that, whilst buying a puppy is a pleasurable and exciting endeavour, it is not something to be taken lightly. Relax...the fun will start when the pup comes home!

Always keep in mind that a puppy is nothing more than a baby in a furry disguise...a baby who is virtually helpless in a human world and who trusts his owner for fulfilment of his basic needs for survival. In addition to water and shelter, your pup needs care, protection, guidance and love. If you are not prepared to commit to this, then you are not prepared to own a dog.

Wait a minute, you say. How hard could this be? All of my neighbours own dogs and they seem to be doing just fine. Why should I have to worry about all of this? Well, you should not worry about it; in

Border Collies are naturally active dogs that require a great deal of exercise to maintain their health and sound bodies.

fact, you will probably find that once your Border Collie pup gets used to his new home, he will fall into his place in the family quite naturally. But it never hurts to emphasise the commitment of dog ownership. With some time and patience, it is really not too difficult to raise a curious and exuberant Border Collie pup to be a well-adjusted and well-mannered adult dog—a dog that could be your most loyal friend.

DID YOU KNOW?

The majority of problems that are commonly seen in young pups will disappear as your dog gets older. However, how you deal with problems when he is young will determine how he reacts to discipline as an adult dog. It is important to establish who is boss (hopefully it will be you!) right away when you are first bonding wiith your dog. This bond will set the tone for the rest of your life together.

PREPARING PUPPY'S PLACE IN YOUR HOME

Researching your breed and finding a breeder are only two aspects of the 'homework' you will have to do before bringing your Border Collie puppy home.

The toughest night with your Border Collie puppy will be the first night, for both the puppy and the family.

You will also have to prepare your home and family for the new addition. Much like you would prepare a nursery for a newborn baby, you will need to designate a place in your home that will be the puppy's own. How you prepare your home will depend on how much freedom the dog will be

DID YOU KNOW?

Taking your dog from the breeder to your home in a car can be a very uncomfortable experience for both of you. The puppy will have been taken from his warm, friendly, safe environ-ment and brought into a strange new environment. An environment that moves! Be prepared for loose bowels, urination, crying, whining and even fear biting. With proper love and encouragement when you arrive home, the stress of the trip should quickly disappear.

DID YOU KNOW?

You should not even think about buying a puppy that looks sick, undernourished, overly frightened or nervous. Sometimes a timid puppy will warm up to you after a 30-minute 'let's-get-acquainted' session.

allowed. Will he be confined to one room or a specific area in the house, or will he be allowed to roam as he pleases? Will he spend most of his time in the house or will he be primarily an outdoor dog? Whatever you decide, you must ensure that he has a place that he can 'call his own.'

When you bring your new puppy into your home, you are bringing him into what will become his home as well. Obviously you did not buy a puppy so that he could take over your house, but in order for a puppy to grow into a stable, well-adjusted dog, he has to feel comfortable in his surroundings. Remember, he is leaving the warmth and security of his mother and littermates, as well as the familiarity of the only place he has ever known, so it is important to make his transition as easy as possible. By preparing a place in your home for the puppy, you are making him feel as welcome as possible in a strange new place. It should not take him long to get used to it,

The Border Collie's coat needs daily brushing and maintenance to stay healthy looking and matt-free.

but the sudden shock of being transplanted is somewhat traumatic for a young pup. Imagine how a small child would feel in the same situation—that is how your puppy must be feeling. It is up to you to reassure him and to let him know, 'Little fellow, you are going to like it here!'

WHAT YOU SHOULD BUY
CRATE
To someone unfamiliar with the use of crates in dog training, it may seem like punishment to shut a dog in a crate, but this is not the case at all. Crates are not cruel—crates have many humane and highly effective uses in dog care and training. For example, crate training is a very popular and very success-ful housebreaking method. A crate can keep your dog safe during travel and, perhaps most importantly, a crate provides

> **DID YOU KNOW?**
> The cost of food must also be mentioned. All dogs need a good quality food with an adequate supply of protein to develop their bones and muscles properly. Most dogs are not picky eaters but unless fed properly they can quickly succumb to skin problems.

Border Collies on their way to a dog show. Whether you own one Border Collie or a truckload, dogs should always be secure in their crates when travelling.

your dog with a place of his own in your home. It serves as a 'doggie bedroom' of sorts—your Border Collie can curl up in his crate when he wants to sleep or when he just needs a break. Many dogs sleep in their crates overnight. When lined with soft blankets and filled with his favourite toys, a crate becomes a cosy pseudo-den for your dog. Like his ancestors, he too will seek out the comfort and retreat of a den—you just happen to be providing him with something a little more luxurious than leaves and twigs lining a dirty ditch.

As far as purchasing a crate, the type that you buy is up to you. It will most likely be one of the two most popular types: wire or fibreglass. There are advantages and disadvantages to each type. For example, a wire crate is more open, allowing the air to flow through and affording

the dog a view of what is going on around him. A fibreglass crate, however, is sturdier and can double as a travel crate since it provides more protection for the dog. The size of the crate is another thing to consider. Puppies do not stay puppies forever—in fact, sometimes it seems as if they grow right before your eyes. A Yorkie-sized crate may be fine for a very young Border Collie pup, but it will not do him much good for long! Unless you have the money and the inclination to buy a new crate every time your pup has a growth spurt, it is better to get one that will accommodate your dog both as a pup and at full size. A medium-size crate will be necessary for a full-grown Border Collie, who stands approximately 21 inches high.

DID YOU KNOW?
The electrical fencing system which forms an invisible fence works on a battery-operated collar that shocks the dog if it gets too close to the buried (or elevated) wire. There are some people who think very highly of this system of controlling a dog's wandering. Keep in mind that the collar has batteries. For safety's sake, replace the batteries every month with the best quality batteries available.

BEDDING

Veterinary bedding in the dog's crate will help the dog feel more at home, and you may also pop in a small blanket. First, the blankets will take the place of the leaves, twigs, etc., that the pup would use in the wild to make a den; the pup can make his own 'burrow' in the crate. Although your pup is far removed from his den-making ancestors, the denning instinct is still a part of his genetic makeup. Second, until you bring your pup home, he has been sleeping amidst the warmth of

PHOTO COURTESY OF DOSKOCIL.

Your pet shop should be able to show you various sizes of crates. Consider the eventual size of your full-grown Border Collie when purchasing a crate.

> **DID YOU KNOW?**
>
> During crate training, you should partition off the section of the crate in which the pup stays. If he is given too big an area, this will hinder your training efforts. Crate training is based on the fact that a dog does not like to soil his sleeping quarters, so it is ineffective to keep a pup in a crate that is so big that he can eliminate in one end and get far enough away from it to sleep. Also, you want to make the crate den-like for the pup. Blankets and a favourite toy will make the crate cosy for the small pup; as he grows, you may want to evict some of his 'roommates' to make more room.
>
> It will take some coaxing at first, but be patient. Given some time to get used to it, your pup will adapt to his new home-within-a-home quite nicely.

his mother and littermates, and whilst a blanket is not the same as a warm, breathing body, it still provides heat and something with which to snuggle. You will want to wash your pup's blankets frequently in case he has an accident in his crate, and replace or remove any blanket that becomes ragged and starts to fall apart.

TOYS

Toys are a must for dogs of all ages, especially for curious playful pups. Puppies are the

41

'sink their teeth into'—everything tastes great!

Border Collie puppies are fairly aggressive chewers and only the hardest, strongest toys should be offered to them. Breeders advise owners to resist stuffed toys, because they can become de-stuffed in no time. The overly excited pup may ingest the stuffing, which is neither digestible nor nutritious.

Similarly, squeaky toys are quite popular, but must be avoided for the Border Collie. Perhaps a squeaky toy can be used as an aid in training, but not for free play. If a pup 'disembowels' one of these, the small plastic squeaker inside can be dangerous if swallowed. Monitor the condition of all your pup's toys carefully and get rid of any that have been

'children' of the dog world, and what child does not love toys? Chew toys provide enjoyment to both dog and owner—your dog will enjoy playing with his favourite toys, whilst you will enjoy the fact that they distract him from your expensive shoes and leather sofa. Puppies love to chew; in fact, chewing is a physical need for pups as they are teething, and everything looks appetising! The full range of your possessions—from old dishrag to Oriental rug—are fair game in the eyes of a teething pup. Puppies are not all that discerning when it comes to finding something to literally

chewed to the point of becoming potentially dangerous.

Be careful of natural bones, which have a tendency to splinter into sharp, dangerous pieces. Also be careful of rawhide, which can turn into pieces that are easy to swallow or into a mushy mess on your carpet.

LEAD

A nylon lead is probably the best option as it is the most resistant to puppy teeth should your pup take a liking to chewing on his lead. Of course, this is a habit that should be nipped in the bud, but if your pup likes to chew on his lead he has a very slim chance of being able to chew through the strong nylon. Nylon leads are also

Unless you want to enter dog shows, you do not need a show dog. Get a sound pup from a reputable breeder.

lightweight, which is good for a young Border Collie who is just getting used to the idea of walking on a lead. For everyday walking and safety purposes, the nylon lead is a good choice. As your pup grows up and gets used to walking on the lead, you may want to purchase a flexible lead. These leads allow you to

PHOTO COURTESY OF MIKKI PET PRODUCTS.

Your pet shop will have a great variety of dog toys that can withstand the wear-and-tear of the Border Collie. NEVER use children's toys for dogs. They are usually not strong enough, or they may contain small components that can be swallowed.

43

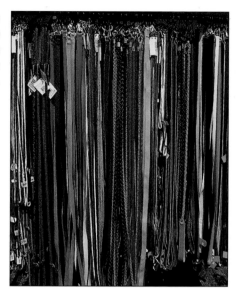

Your local pet shop should have a large variety of leads suitable for your Border Collie.

around the pup's neck. You should be able to fit a finger between the pup and the collar. It may take some time for your pup to get used to wearing the collar, but soon he will not even notice that it is there. Choke collars are made for training, but should only be used by an experienced handler.

FOOD AND WATER BOWLS

Your pup will need two bowls, one for food and one for water. You may want two sets of bowls, one for inside and one for outside, depending on where the dog will be fed and where he will be spending most of his time. Stainless steel or sturdy plastic bowls are popular choices. Plastic bowls are more chewable. Dogs tend not to chew on the steel variety, which can be sterilised. It is important to buy

extend the length to give the dog a broader area to explore or to shorten the length to keep the close to you. Of course there are special leads for training purposes, and specially made leather harnesses for the working Border Collies, but these are not necessary for routine walks.

COLLAR

Your pup should get used to wearing a collar all the time since you will want to attach his ID tags to it. You have to attach the lead to something! A lightweight nylon collar is a good choice; make sure that it fits snugly enough so that the pup cannot wriggle out of it, but is loose enough so that it will not be uncomfortably tight

DID YOU KNOW?

Training your puppy takes much patience and can be frustrating at times, but you should see results from your efforts. If you have a puppy that seems untrainable, take him to a trainer or behaviourist. The dog may have a personality problem that requires the help of a professional, or perhaps you need help in learning how to train your dog.

sturdy bowls since anything is in danger of being chewed by puppy teeth and you do not want your dog to be constantly chewing apart his bowl (for his safety and for your purse!).

CLEANING SUPPLIES

Until a pup is housetrained you will be doing a lot of cleaning. Accidents will occur, which is okay in the beginning because the puppy does not know any better. All you can do is be prepared to clean up any 'accidents.' Old rags, towels, newspapers and a safe disinfectant are good to have on hand.

BEYOND THE BASICS

The items previously discussed are the bare necessities. You will find out what else you need as you go along—grooming supplies, flea/tick protection, baby gates to partition a room, etc. These things will vary depending on your situation but it is important that you have everything you need to feed and make your Border Collie comfortable in his first few days at home.

PUPPY-PROOFING YOUR HOME

Aside from making sure that your Border Collie will be comfortable in your home, you also have to make sure that your home is safe for your Border

There are many kinds of bowls available at your local pet shop. Your Border Collie needs sturdy bowls for food and water.

Stainless steel bowls are usually the strongest variety of dog bowls. These bowls cannot be chewed and can be readily sanitised. Plastic bowls do not last as long and are very chewable.

Pet shops usually have various kinds of equipment to aid you in cleaning up the garden after your dog has relieved himself.

Collie. This means taking precautions that your pup will not get into anything he should not get into and that there is nothing within his reach that may harm him should he sniff it, chew it, inspect it, etc. This probably seems obvious since, whilst you are primarily concerned with your pup's safety, at the same time you do not want your belongings to be ruined. Breakables should be placed out of reach if your dog is to have full run of the house. If he is to be limited to certain places within the house, keep any potentially dangerous items in the 'off-limits' areas. An electrical cord can pose a danger should the puppy decide to taste it—and who is going to convince a pup that it would not make a great chew toy? Cords should be fastened tightly against the wall. If your dog is going to spend time in a crate, make sure that there is nothing near his crate that he can reach if he sticks his curious little

nose or paws through the openings. Just as you would with a child, keep all household cleaners and chemicals where the pup cannot get to them.

It is also important to make sure that the outside of your home is safe. Of course your puppy should never be unsupervised, but a pup let loose in the garden will want to run and explore, and he should be granted that freedom. Do not let a fence give you a false sense of security; you would be surprised how crafty (and persistent) a dog can be in figuring out how to dig under and squeeze his way through small holes, or to jump or climb over a fence. The remedy is to make the fence high enough so

Border Collie pups love to run and explore. Ensure your pup's safety in open areas by keeping him on a lead.

that it really is impossible for your dog to get over it (about 3 metres should suffice), and well embedded into the ground. Be sure to repair or secure any gaps in the fence. Check the fence periodically to ensure that it is in good shape and make repairs as needed; a very determined pup may return to the same spot to 'work on it' until he is able to get through.

FIRST TRIP TO THE VET
You have picked out your puppy, and your home and family are ready. Now all you have to do is collect your Border Collie from the breeder and the

fun begins, right? Well…not so fast. Something else you need to prepare is your pup's first trip to the veterinary surgeon. Perhaps the breeder can recommend someone in the area that specialises in Border Collies, or maybe you know some other Border Collie owners who can suggest a good vet. Either way, you should have an appointment arranged for your pup before you pick him up and plan on taking him for an examination before bringing him home.

The pup's first visit will consist of an overall examination to make sure that the pup

47

The average income for American veterinary surgeons, broken into categories. This is a good indicator of how much money pet owners spend for their animals' medical care.

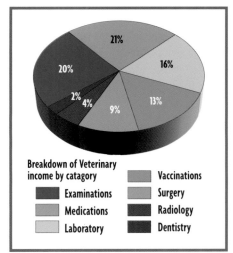

Breakdown of Veterinary income by catagory

Examinations	Vaccinations
Medications	Surgery
Laboratory	Radiology
	Dentistry

21% 16% 20% 2% 4% 9% 13%

does not have any problems that are not apparent to the eye. The veterinary surgeon will also set up a schedule for the pup's vaccinations; the breeder will inform you of which ones the pup has already received and the vet can continue from there.

INTRODUCTION TO THE FAMILY

Everyone in the house will be excited about the puppy coming home and will want to pet him and play with him, but it is best to make the introduction low-key so as not to overwhelm the puppy. He is apprehensive already. It is the first time he has been separated from his mother and the breeder, and the ride to your home is likely the first time he has been in an auto. The last thing you want to do is smother

him, as this will only frighten him further. This is not to say that human contact is not extremely necessary at this stage, because this is the time when a connection between the pup and his human family is formed. Gentle petting and soothing words should help console him, as well as just putting him down and letting him explore on his own (under your watchful eye, of course).

The pup may approach the family members or may busy himself with exploring for a while. Gradually, each person should spend some time with the pup, one at a time, crouching down to get as close to the pup's level as possible and letting him sniff their hands and petting him gently. He definitely needs human attention and he needs to be touched—this is how to form an immediate bond. Just remember that the pup is experiencing a lot of things for the first time, at the same time. There are new people, new noises, new smells, and new things to investigate: so be gentle, be affectionate, and be as comforting as you can be.

YOUR PUP'S FIRST NIGHT HOME

You have travelled home with your new charge safely in his basket or crate. He's been to the vet for a thorough check-over;

he's been weighed, his papers examined; perhaps he's even been vaccinated and wormed as well. He's met the family, licked the whole family, including the excited children and the less-than-happy cat. He's explored his area, his new bed, the garden and anywhere else he's been permitted. He's eaten his first meal at home and relieved himself in the proper place. He's heard lots of new sounds, smelled new friends and seen more of the outside world than ever before.

That was just the first day! He's tuckered out and is ready for bed…or so you think!

It's puppy's first night and you are ready to say 'Good night'—keep in mind that this is puppy's first night ever to be sleeping alone. His dam and littermates are no longer at paw's length and he's a bit scared, cold and lonely. Be reassuring to your new family member. This is not the time to spoil him and give in to his inevitable whining.

Puppies whine. They whine to let the others know where they are and hopefully to get company out of it. Place your pup in his new bed or crate in his room and close the door. Mercifully, he may fall asleep without a peep. If the inevitable occurs, ignore the whining: he is fine. Be strong and keep his interest in mind. Do not allow your heart to become guilty and visit the pup. He will fall asleep.

Many breeders recommend placing a piece of bedding from his former homestead in his new bed so that he recognises the scent of his littermates.

Kissing your Border Collie, or any dog, on the mouth is quite unsanitary.

Others still advise placing a hot water bottle in his bed for warmth. This latter may be a good idea provided the pup doesn't attempt to suckle—he'll get good and wet and may not fall asleep so fast.

You should shower your Border Collie with love and affection. Kissing on the mouth, however, is not recommended for health reasons.

Puppy's first night can be somewhat stressful for the pup and his new family. Remember that you are setting the tone of nighttime at your house. Unless you want to play with your pup

'You can't teach an old dog new tricks' is an untrue expression, but it is easier to train a pup.

every evening at 10 p.m., midnight and 2 a.m., don't initiate the habit. Your family will thank you, and so will your pup!

PREVENTING PUPPY PROBLEMS

SOCIALISATION

Now that you have done all of the preparatory work and have helped your pup get accustomed to his new home and family, it is about time for you to have some fun! Socialising your Border Collie pup gives you the opportunity to show off your new friend, and your pup gets to reap the benefits of being an adorable furry creature that people will want to pet and, in general, think is absolutely precious!

Besides getting to know his new family, your puppy should be exposed to other people, animals and situations. This will help him become well adjusted as he grows up and less prone to being timid or fearful of the new things he will encounter. Your pup's socialisation began at the breeder's but now it is your responsibility to continue it. The socialisation he receives up until the age of 12 weeks is the most critical, as this is the time when he forms his impressions of the outside world. Be especially careful during the eight-to-ten-week period, also known as the fear period. The interaction he receives during this time should be gentle and reassuring. Lack of socialisation can manifest itself in fear and aggression as the dog grows up. He needs lots of human contact, affection, handling and exposure to other animals.

Once your pup

DID YOU KNOW?

Thorough socialisation includes not only meeting new people but also being introduced to new experiences such as riding in the auto, having his coat brushed, hearing the television, walking in a crowd—the list is endless. The more your pup experiences, and the more positive the experiences are, the less of a shock and the less scary it will be for your pup to encounter new things.

DID YOU KNOW?

It will take at least two weeks for your puppy to become accustomed to his new surroundings. Give him lots of love, attention, handling, frequent opportunities to relieve himself, a diet he likes to eat and a place he can call his own.

has received his necessary vaccinations, feel free to take him out and about (on his lead, of course). Walk him around the neighbourhood, take him on your daily errands, let people pet him, let him meet other dogs and pets, etc. Puppies do not have to try to make friends; there will be no shortage of people who will want to introduce themselves. Just make sure that you carefully supervise each meeting. If the neighbourhood children want to say hello, for example, that is great—children and pups most often make great companions. Sometimes an excited child can unintentionally handle a pup too roughly, or an overzealous pup can playfully nip a little too hard. You want to make socialisation experiences positive ones. What a pup learns during this very formative stage will impact his attitude toward future encounters. You want your dog to be comfortable around everyone. A pup that has a bad experience with a child may grow up to be a dog that is shy around or aggressive toward children.

CONSISTENCY IN TRAINING

Dogs, being pack animals, naturally need a leader, or else they try to establish dominance in their packs. When you bring a dog into your family, the choice of who becomes the leader and who becomes the 'pack' is entirely up to you! Your pup's intuitive quest for dominance, coupled with the fact that it is nearly impossible to look at an adorable Border Collie pup, with his 'puppy-dog' eyes and his too-big-for-his-head-still-floppy ears, and not cave in, give the pup almost an unfair advantage in getting the upper hand! A pup will definitely test the waters to see what he can and cannot do. Do not give in to those pleading eyes—stand your ground when it comes to disciplining the pup and make sure that all family members do the same. It will only confuse the pup when Mother tells him to get off the couch when he is used to sitting up there with Father to watch the nightly news. Avoid discrepancies by having all members of the household decide on the rules before the pup even comes home…and be consistent in enforcing them! Early training shapes the dog's personality, so you cannot be unclear in what you expect.

COMMON PUPPY PROBLEMS
The best way to prevent puppy problems is to be proactive in stopping an undesirable behaviour as soon as it starts.

A favourite toy keeps the pup occupied and will distract him from inappropriate chewing.

The old saying 'You can't teach an old dog new tricks' does not necessarily hold true, but it is true that it is much easier to discourage bad behaviour in a young developing pup than to wait until the pup's bad behaviour becomes the adult dog's bad habit. There are some problems that are especially prevalent in puppies as they develop.

NIPPING
As puppies start to teethe, they feel the need to sink their teeth into anything available... unfortunately that includes your fingers, arms, hair, and toes. You may find this behaviour cute for the first five seconds...until you feel just how sharp those puppy teeth are. This is something you want to discourage immediately and consistently with a firm 'No!' (or whatever number of firm 'No's' it takes for him to understand that you mean business). Then replace your finger with an appropriate chew toy. Whilst this behaviour is merely annoying when the dog is young, it can become dangerous as your Border Collie's adult teeth grow in and his jaws develop, and he continues to think it is okay to gnaw on human appendages. Your Border Collie does not mean any harm with a friendly nip, but he also does not know his own strength.

CRYING/WHINING
Your pup will often cry, whine, whimper, howl or make some type of commotion when he is left alone. This is basically his way of calling out for attention to make sure that you know he is there and that you have not forgotten about him. He feels insecure when he is left alone, when you are out of the house and he is in his crate or when you are in another part of the house and he cannot see you. The noise he is making is an expression of the anxiety he feels at being alone, so he needs to be taught that being alone is okay. You are not actually training the dog to stop making noise, you are training him to feel comfortable when he is alone and

Playtime! The puppies have been tattooed for identification purposes (enhanced for this photograph). Breeders commonly have the whole litter tattooed as early as six or eight weeks.

your help, and it will not be so traumatic for him when you are not around. You may want to leave the radio on softly when you leave the house; the sound of human voices may be comforting to him.

thus removing the need for him to make the noise. This is where the crate filled with cosy blankets and a toy comes in handy. You want to know that he is safe when you are not there to supervise, and you know that he will be safe in his crate rather than roaming freely about the house. In order for the pup to stay in his crate without making a fuss, he needs to be comfortable in his crate. On that note, it is extremely important that the crate is never used as a form of punishment, or the pup will have a negative association with the crate.

Accustom the pup to the crate in short, gradually increasing time intervals in which you put him in the crate, maybe with a treat, and stay in the room with him. If he cries or makes a fuss, do not go to him, but stay in his sight. Gradually he will realise that staying in his crate is all right without

DID YOU KNOW?

Chewing goes hand in hand with nipping in the sense that a teething puppy is always looking for a way to soothe his aching gums. In this case, instead of chewing on you, he may have taken a liking to your favourite shoe or something else on which he should not be chewing. Again, realise that this is a normal canine behaviour that does not need to be discouraged, only redirected. Your pup just needs to be taught what is acceptable to chew on and what is off limits. Consistently tell him NO when you catch him chewing on something forbidden and give him a chew toy. Conversely, praise him when you catch him chewing on something appropriate. In this way you are discouraging the inappropriate behaviour and reinforcing the desired behaviour. The puppy chewing should stop after his adult teeth have come in, but an adult dog continues to chew for various reasons—perhaps because he is bored, perhaps to relieve tension or perhaps he just likes to chew. That is why it is important to redirect his chewing when he is still young.

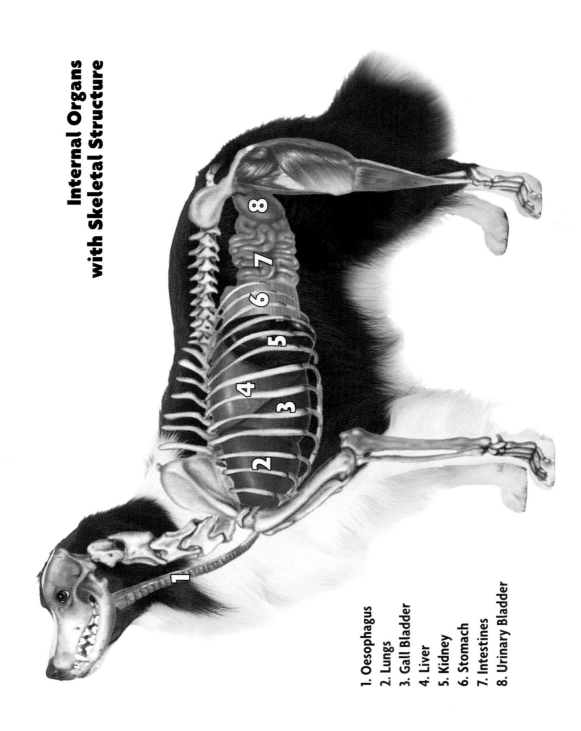

Internal Organs
with Skeletal Structure

1. Oesophagus
2. Lungs
3. Gall Bladder
4. Liver
5. Kidney
6. Stomach
7. Intestines
8. Urinary Bladder

DIETARY AND FEEDING CONSIDERATIONS

You have probably heard it a thousand times, 'you are what you eat.' Believe it or not, it's very true. Dogs are what you feed them because they have little choice in the matter. Even those people who truly want to feed their dogs the best often cannot do so because they do not know which foods are best for their dog.

Dog foods are produced in three basic types: dry, semi-moist and tinned. Dry foods are the choice of the cost conscious because they are much less expensive than semi-moist and canned. Dry foods contain the least fat and the most preservatives. Most tinned foods are 60–70-percent water, whilst semi-moist foods are so full of sugar that they are the least preferred by owners, though dogs welcome them (as a child does sweets).

Three stages of development must be considered when selecting a diet for your dog: the puppy stage, the mid-age or adult stage and the senior age or geriatric stage.

PUPPY STAGE

Puppies have a natural instinct to suck milk from their mother's teats. They exhibit this behaviour from the first moments of their lives. If they

DID YOU KNOW?

Selecting the best dry dog food is difficult. There is no majority consensus among veterinary scientists as to the value of nutrient analyses (protein, fat, fibre, moisture, ash, cholesterol, minerals, etc.). All agree that feeding trials are what matters, but you also have to consider the individual dog. Its weight, age, activity and what pleases its taste all must be considered. It is probably best to take the advice of your veterinary surgeon. Every dog's dietary requirements vary, even during the lifetime of a particular dog.

If your dog is fed a good dry food, it does not require supplements of meat or vegetables. Dogs do appreciate a little variety in their diets so you may choose to stay with the same brand, but vary the flavour. Alternatively you may wish to add a little flavoured stock to give a difference to the taste.

don't suckle within a short while, the breeder attempts to put them onto their mother's nipple. A newborn's failure to suckle often requires that the breeder handfeed the pup under the guidance of a veterinary surgeon. This involves a baby bottle and a special formula. Their mother's milk is much better than any formula because it contains colostrum, a sort of antibiotic milk that protects the puppy during the first eight to ten weeks of their lives.

Puppies should be allowed to nurse for six weeks and they

DID YOU KNOW?

Dog food must be at room tempera-ture, neither too hot nor too cold. Fresh water, changed daily and served in a clean bowl, is mandatory, especially when feeding dry food.

Never feed your dog from the table while you are eating. Never feed your dog left-overs from your own meal. They usually contain too much fat and too much seasoning.

Dogs must chew their food. Hard pellets are excellent; soups and slurries are to be avoided.

Don't add left-overs or any extras to normal dog food. The normal food is usually balanced and adding something extra destroys the balance.

Except for age-related changes, dogs do not require dietary variations. They can be fed the same diet, day after day, without their becoming bored or ill.

DID YOU KNOW?

A good test for proper diet is the colour, odour, and firmness of your dog's stool. A healthy dog usually produces three semi-hard stools per day. The stools should have no unpleasant odour. They should be the same colour from excretion to excretion.

should be slowly weaned away from their mother by introducing small portions of tinned meat after they are about one month old. Then dry food is gradually added to the puppies' portions over the next few weeks.

By the time they are eight weeks old, they should be completely weaned and fed solely a puppy dry food. During this weaning period, their diet is most important as the puppy grows fastest during its first year of life.

Border Collie pups should be fed three meals per day when they are six to eight weeks of age. At eight weeks, the pup can be fed twice per day. Fussy eaters may require an additional smaller meal to maintain a good weight. Many breeders recommend feeding Border Collie puppies brown bread and milk. Should the owner not wish to purchase real milk, a substi-tute intended for goats is preferred to a human powder substitute. Never offer puppies sweet cake or white bread. Adding some vegetation to the diet occasionally is excellent for most dogs. Canines are omnivores, which means that they cannot subsist on meat alone.

Puppy diets should be balanced for your dog's needs, and supplements of vitamins, minerals and protein should not be necessary. Since Border Collie puppies become increasingly active as they grow, as is true with most puppies, they require more food for their size than do adults. Energy foods, high in protein, will give your puppy the power he needs. Whilst the pup should not have a fat tummy, you can judge his nourishment by his appearance: shiny coat, strong legs, alert, happy disposition, etc.

ADULT DIETS

A dog is considered an adult when it has stopped growing in height and/or length. Do not consider the dog's weight when

A Border Collie is not considered an adult until he stops growing.

the decision is made to switch from a puppy diet to a maintenance diet. Again you should rely upon your veterinary surgeon to recommend an acceptable maintenance diet.

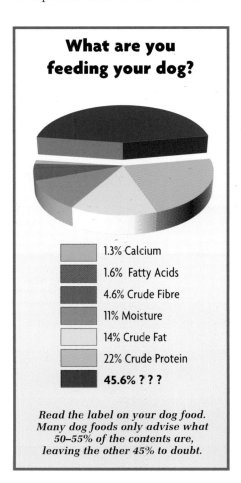

What are you feeding your dog?

	1.3% Calcium
	1.6% Fatty Acids
	4.6% Crude Fibre
	11% Moisture
	14% Crude Fat
	22% Crude Protein
	45.6% ? ? ?

Read the label on your dog food. Many dog foods only advise what 50–55% of the contents are, leaving the other 45% to doubt.

DID YOU KNOW?

You must store your dry dog food carefully. Open packages of dog food quickly lose their vitamin value, usually within 90 days of being opened. Mould spores and vermin could also contaminate the food.

Border Collies must have balanced diets at every age.

Major dog food manufacturers specialise in this type of food and it is just necessary for you to select the one best suited to your dog's needs. Active dogs like the Border Collie insist upon quality diets: quality, not quantity. Protein is important to the diet. Owners are warned against diets high in maize, which lacks in vitamin B and can cause 'black tongue' in dogs.

A Border Collie is fully mature around 12 months of age, though it often takes another 12 to 18 months for dog to reach its peak as a performance animal.

DID YOU KNOW?

Many adult diets are based on grain. There is nothing wrong with this as long as it does not contain soy meal. Diets based on soy often cause flatulence (passing gas).

Grain-based diets are almost always the least expensive and a good grain diet is just as good as the most expensive diet containing animal protein.

There are many cases, however, when your dog might require a special diet. These special requirements should only be recommended by your veterinary surgeon.

SENIOR DIETS

As dogs get older, their metabolism changes. The older dog usually exercises less, moves more slowly and sleeps more. This change in lifestyle and physiological performance requires a change in diet. Since these changes take place slowly, they might not be recognisable. What is easily recognisable is weight gain. By continually feeding your dog an adult maintenance diet when it is slowing down metabolically, your dog will gain weight. Obesity in an older dog compounds the health problems that already accompany old age.

As your dog gets older, few of their organs function up to par. The kidneys slow down and the intestines become less efficient. These age-related factors are best handled with a change in diet and a change in feeding schedule to give smaller portions that are more easily digested.

There is no single best diet for every older dog. Whilst many dogs do well on light or senior diets, other dogs do better on puppy diets or other special premium diets such as lamb and rice.

Be sensitive to your senior Border Collie's diet and this will help control other problems that may arise with your old friend.

WATER

Just as your dog needs proper nutrition from his food, water is an essential 'nutrient' as well. Water keeps the dog's body properly hydrated and promotes normal function of the body's systems. During housebreaking it is necessary to keep an eye on how much water your Border Collie is drinking, but once he is reliably trained he should have access to clean fresh water at all times. Make sure that the dog's water bowl is clean, and change the water often.

EXERCISE

All dogs require some form of exercise, regardless of breed. A sedentary lifestyle is as harmful to a dog as it is to a person, but for the Border Collie it's hell! The Border Collie is indeed a very active breed that requires more exercise than most breeds. The pet Border Collie does not have the avantage of real work—the only true exercise for a Border Collie—herding sheep up and down hills for a few hours keeps the dog fit and active. Owners of the non-farmer/non-shepherd type will require great lengths to keep their Border Collies mentally and physically balanced. Regular walks (an hour twice per day), play sessions in the garden, and letting the dog run free in the garden under your supervision are all good exercise for the

Border Collies require more exercise than average dogs. Whilst not all Border Collies will welcome a swim in a stream, many will quite enjoy it.

Border Collie. Not only is exercise essential to keep the Border Collie's body fit, it is essential to his mental well being. A bored dog will find something to do, which often manifests itself in some type of destructive behaviour. In this sense, it is essential for the owner's mental

Grooming your Border Collie should be a pleasure, not a chore.

well being as well! Amongst dogs, the Border Collie needs more exercise and stimulation than any other breed. Without good outlets for his abundant energy, the Border Collie will suffer a thousand boring deaths!

GROOMING
BRUSHING

A natural bristle brush or a hound glove can be used for regular routine brushing. Daily brushing is effective for

59

Your Border Collie should be given at least a five-minute brushing every day. This daily contact reinforces the human-dog bonding process.

removing dead hair and stimulating the dog's natural oils to add shine and a healthy look to the coat. A Border Collie with a short or medium-length coat will require a five-minute once-over to keep it looking its shiny best. Regular grooming sessions are also a good way to spend time with your dog. Many dogs grow to like the feel of being brushed and will enjoy the daily routine.

Border Collies with longer, fuller coats will require a bit more attention, especially when they are casting their coats. 'Cots' can form at the base of the ear and on the legs if the dog is not brushed every day or every other day.

Your Border Collie requires a thorough pre-bath brushing to detangle the coat before wetting it.

BATHING

Dogs do not need to be bathed as often as humans, but regular bathing is essential for healthy skin and a healthy, shiny coat. Again, like most anything, if you accustom your pup to being bathed as a puppy, it will be second nature by the time he grows up. You want your dog to be at ease in the bath or else it could end up a wet, soapy, messy ordeal for both of you!

DID YOU KNOW?

The use of human soap products like shampoo, bubble bath and hand soap can be damaging to a dog's coat and skin. Human products are too strong and remove the protective oils coating the dog's hair and skin (making him water-resistant). Use only shampoo made especially for dogs and you may like to use a medicated shampoo which will always help to keep external parasites at bay.

Brush your Border Collie thoroughly before wetting his coat. This will get rid of most matts and tangles, which are harder to remove when the coat is wet. Make sure that your dog has a good non-slip surface to stand on. Begin by wetting the dog's coat. A shower or hose attachment is necessary for thoroughly wetting and rinsing the coat. Check the water temperature to make sure that it is neither too hot nor too cold.

Next, apply shampoo to the dog's coat and work it into a good lather. You should purchase a shampoo that is made for dogs. Do not use a product made for human hair. Wash the head last; you do not want shampoo to drip into the dog's eyes whilst you are washing the rest of his body. Work the shampoo all the way down to the skin. You can use this opportunity to check the skin for any bumps, bites or other abnormalities. Do not neglect any area of the body—get all of the hard-to-reach places.

Once the dog has been thoroughly shampooed, he requires an equally thorough rinsing. Shampoo left in the coat can be irritating to the skin. Protect his eyes from the shampoo by shielding them with your hand and directing the flow of water in the opposite direction. You should also avoid getting water in the ear canal. Be prepared for your

DID YOU KNOW?

Once you are sure that the dog is thoroughly rinsed, squeeze the excess water out of the coat with your hand and dry him with a

heavy towel. You may choose to use a blaster on his coat or just let it dry naturally. In cold weather, never allow your dog outside with a wet coat.

There are 'dry bath' products on the market, which are sprays and powders intended for spot cleaning, that can be used between regular baths if necessary. They are not substitutes for regular baths, but they are easy to use for touch-ups as they do not require rinsing.

dog to shake out his coat—you might want to stand back, but make sure you have a hold on the dog to keep him from running through the house.

EAR CLEANING

The ears should be kept clean and any excess hair inside the ear should be trimmed. Ears can be cleaned with cotton wipes and

After your Border Collie has been bathed and dried, the coat should be combed thoroughly.

61

Ears should be gently and carefully cleaned. Look for ear mites or other signs of irritation or infection.

Your local pet shop will carry a variety of grooming tools.

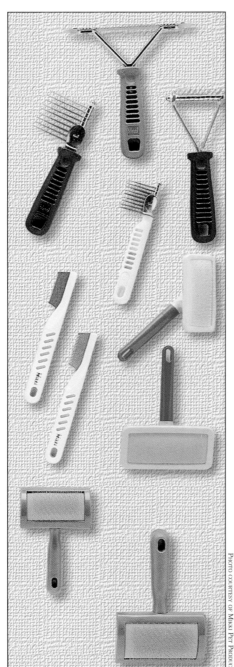

Your Border Collie's ears should be cleaned weekly. Excess hairs inside the ear should be trimmed.

PHOTO COURTESY OF MIKKI PET PRODUCTS.

special cleaner or ear powder made especially for dogs. Be on the lookout for any signs of infection or ear mite infestation. If your Border Collie has been shaking his head or scratching at his ears frequently, this usually indicates a problem. If his ears have an unusual odour, this is a sure sign of mite infestation or infection, and a signal to have his ears checked by the veterinary surgeon.

NAIL CLIPPING

Your Border Collie should be accustomed to having his nails trimmed at an early age, since it

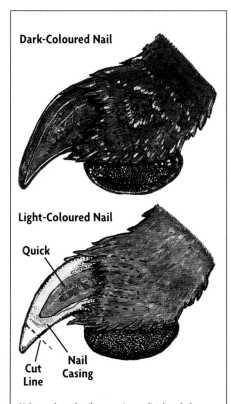

Dark-Coloured Nail

Light-Coloured Nail

Quick

Cut Line

Nail Casing

Lighter coloured nails are easier to clip than darker ones because the quick is more easily visible. To be safe, only clip off the sharp tip of the nails a little at a time.

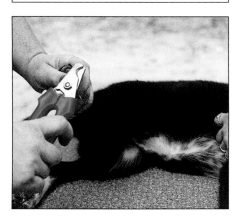

will be part of your maintenance routine throughout his life. More than mere cosmetics, a dog with unsightly long nails can cause injury if he jumps up or if he scratches someone unintentionally. For the dog's health, its long nails have more chance of ripping and bleeding as well as causing the feet to splay. A good rule of thumb is that if you can hear your dog's nails clicking on the floor when he walks, his nails are too long.

Before you start cutting, make sure you can identify the 'quick' in each nail. The quick is a blood vessel that runs through the centre of each nail and grows rather close to the end. It will bleed if accidentally cut, which

DID YOU KNOW?
How much grooming equipment you purchase will depend on how much grooming you are going to do. Here are some basics:

- Natural bristle brush
- Slicker brush
- Metal comb
- Scissors
- Blaster
- Rubber mat
- Dog shampoo
- Spray hose attachment
- Ear cleaner
- Cotton buds
- Towels
- Nail clippers

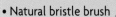

Your local pet shop sells nail clippers especially made for dogs' nails. The guillotine-type is the most preferred.

You can use trimming scissors to cut away the excess hair growth on the foot to keep it looking tidy.

will be quite painful for the dog as it contains nerve endings. Keep some type of clotting agent on hand, such as a styptic pencil or styptic powder (the type used for shaving). This will stop the bleeding quickly when applied to the end of the cut nail. Do not panic if this happens, just stop the bleeding and talk soothingly to your dog. Once he has calmed down, move on to the next nail. It is better to clip a little at a time, particularly with black-nailed dogs.

Hold your pup steady as you begin trimming his nails; you do not want him to make any sudden movements or run away. Talk to him soothingly and stroke his fur as you clip. Holding his foot in your hand, simply take off the end of each nail in one quick clip. You can purchase nail clippers that are specially made for dogs; you can probably find them wherever you buy pet or grooming supplies.

TRAVELLING WITH YOUR DOG
CAR TRAVEL
You should accustom your Border Collie to riding in a car at an early age. You may or may not take him in the car often, but at the very least he will need to go to the vet and you do not want these trips to be traumatic for the dog or a big hassle for you. The safest way for a dog to ride in the car is in his crate. If he uses a fibreglass crate in the house, you can use the same crate for travel. Wire crates can be used for travel, but fibreglass or wooden crates are safer.

Put the pup in the crate and see how he reacts. If he seems uneasy, you can have a passenger hold

DID YOU KNOW?
A dog that spends a lot of time outside on a hard surface such as cement or pavement will have his nails naturally worn down and may not need to have them trimmed as often, except maybe in the colder months when he is not outside as much. Regardless, it is best to get your dog accustomed to this procedure at an early age so that he is used to it. Some dogs are especially sensitive about having their feet touched, but if a dog has experienced it since he was young, he should not be bothered by it.

him on his lap whilst you drive. Another option is a specially made safety harness for dogs, which straps the dog in much like a seat belt. Do not let the dog roam loose in the vehicle—this is very dangerous! If you should stop short, your dog can be thrown and injured. If the dog

starts climbing on you and pestering you whilst you are driving, you will not be able to concentrate on the road. It is an unsafe situation for everyone—human and canine.

For long trips, be prepared to stop to let the dog relieve himself. Bring along whatever you need to clean up after him. You should bring along some old towels and rags, should he have an accident in the car or become carsick.

AIR TRAVEL

If bringing your dog on a flight, you will have to contact the airline to make special arrangements. It is rather common for dogs to travel by air, but advance permission is usually required. The dog will be required to travel in a fibreglass crate; you may be able to use your own or the airline can usually supply one. To help the dog be at ease, put one of his favourite toys in the crate with him. Do not feed the dog for at least six hours

65

Dogs, during any mode of travel, should be restrained. During a car ride, Border Collies are safer in their individual crates.

of the plane than human passengers, and, although transporting animals is routine for large airlines, there is always the slight risk of getting separated from your dog.

DID YOU KNOW?
The most extensive travel you do with your dog may be limited to trips to the veterinary surgeon's office—or you may decide to bring him along for long distances when the family goes on holiday. Whichever the case, it is important to consider your dog's safety while travelling.

before the trip to minimise his need to relieve himself. However, certain regulations specify that water must always be made available to the dog in the crate.

Make sure your dog is properly identified and that your contact information appears on his ID tags and on his crate. Animals travel in a different area

BOARDING
So you want to take a family holiday—and you want to include all members of the family. You would probably make arrangements for accommodations ahead of time anyway, but this is especially important when travelling with a dog. You do not want to make an overnight stop at the only place around for miles and find out that they do not allow dogs. Also, you do not want to reserve a place for your family without confirming that you are travelling with a dog because if it is against their policy you may not have a place to stay.

Alternatively, if you are travelling and choose not to bring your Border Collie, you

DID YOU KNOW?
Never leave your dog alone in the car. In hot weather your dog can die from the high temperature inside a closed vehicle; even a car parked in the shade can heat up very quickly. Leaving the window open is dangerous as well since the dog can hurt himself trying to get out.

will have to make arrangements for him whilst you are away. Some options are to bring him to a neighbour's house to stay whilst you are gone, to have a trusted neighbour stop by often or stay at your house, or bring your dog to a reputable boarding kennel. If you choose to board him at a kennel, you

A tattoo is usually done in a relatively hair-free spot such as the inside of the hind leg.

should stop by to see the facility and where the dogs are kept to make sure that it is clean. Talk to some of the employees and see how they treat the dogs—do they spend time with the dogs, play with them, exercise them, etc.? You know that your Border Collie will not be happy unless he gets regular activity. Also find out the kennel's policy on vaccinations and what they require. This is for all of the dogs' safety, since when dogs are kept together, there is a greater

risk of diseases being passed from dog to dog. Many veterinary surgeons offer boarding facilities; this is another option.

IDENTIFICATION
Your Border Collie is your valued companion and friend. That is why you always keep a close eye on him and you have made sure that he cannot escape from the garden or wriggle out of his collar and run away from you. However, accidents can happen and there may come a time when your dog unexpectedly gets separated from you. If this unfortunate event should occur, the first thing on your mind will be finding him. Proper identification, including an ID tag, a tattoo, and possibly a microchip, will increase the chances of his being returned to you safely and quickly.

Proper boarding facilities should have adequate space in which the Border Collies can be exercised.

A soft patch of dirt looks like a good spot to dig! If your pup has tendencies to dig, correct this behaviour early on so that he will not grow up to terrorise your flower patches.

Living with an untrained dog is a lot like owning a piano that you do not know how to play—it is a nice object to look at but it does not do much more than that to bring you pleasure. Now try taking piano lessons and suddenly the piano comes alive and brings forth magical sounds and rhythms that set your heart singing and your body swaying.

The same is true with your Border Collie. At first you enjoy seeing him around the house. He does not do much with you other than to need food, water and exercise. Come to think of it, he does not bring you much joy, either. He is a big responsibility with a very small return. Often he develops unacceptable behaviours that annoy and/or infuriate you to say nothing of bad habits that may end up costing you great sums of money. Not a good thing!

Now train your Border Collie. Enrol in an obedience class. Teach him good manners as you learn how and why he behaves the way he does. Find out how to communicate with your dog and how to recognise and understand his communications with you. Suddenly the dog takes on a new role in your life—he is smart, interesting, well behaved and fun to be with. He demonstrates his bond of devotion to you daily. In other words, your Border Collie does wonders for your ego because he constantly reminds you that you are not only his leader, you are his hero!

DID YOU KNOW?
Dogs are the most honourable animals in existence. They consider another species (humans) as their own. They interface with you. You are their leader. Puppies perceive children to be on their level: their actions around small children are different than their behaviour around their adult masters.

DID YOU KNOW?

Dogs are sensitive to their master's moods and emotions. Use your voice wisely when communicating with your dog. Never raise your voice at your dog unless you are angry and trying to correct him. 'Barking' at your dog can become as meaningless as 'dogspeak' is to you. Think before you bark!

ownership. For example, training dogs when they are puppies results in the highest rate of success in developing well-mannered and well-adjusted adult dogs. Training an older dog, from six months to six years of age, can produce almost equal results providing that the owner accepts the dog's slower rate of learning capability and is willing

Miraculous things have happened—you have a wonderful dog (even your family and friends have noticed the transformation!) and you feel good about yourself.

It's difficult to imagine a Border Collie without a proper education. Given the immense talents of our breed, both physical and mental, it would be a great pity not to provide your Border Collie with the education he rightly deserves. Without stimulation and challenges, the Border Collie will die! Of all breeds of dogs, here is the ultimate student, the most willing helpmate on the planet, a dog for all seasons!

Those involved with teaching dog obedience and counselling owners about their dogs' behaviour have discovered some interesting facts about dog

Puppies are most trainable between 2 and 4 months old.

to work patiently to help the dog succeed at developing to his fullest potential. Unfortunately, many owners of untrained adult dogs lack the patience factor, so they do not persist until their dogs are successful at learning particular behaviours.

Training a puppy, aged 8 to 16 weeks (20 weeks at the most)

Border Collies derived from working-dog stock, as opposed to show-dog stock, are more likely to demonstrate an early aptitude for shepherding.

69

The entire family should take part in training the Border Collie. Children must learn their responsibilities concerning the care and safety of their pets.

approach of a stranger, he will respond accordingly.

Once the puppy begins to produce hormones, his natural curiosity emerges and he begins to investigate the world around him. It is at this time when you may notice that the untrained dog begins to wander away from you and even ignore your commands to stay close. When this behaviour becomes a problem, the owner has two choices: get rid of the dog or

is like working with a dry sponge in a pool of water. The pup soaks up whatever you show him and constantly looks for more things to do and learn. At this early age, his body is not yet producing hormones, and therein lies the reason for such a high rate of success. Without hormones, he is focused on his owners and not particularly interested in investigating other places, dogs, people, etc. You are his leader: his provider of food, water, shelter and security. He latches onto you and wants to stay close. He will usually follow you from room to room, will not let you out of his sight when you are outdoors with him, and respond in like manner to the people and animals you encounter. If you greet a friend warmly, he will be happy to greet the person as well. If, however, you are hesitant, even anxious, about the

train him. It is strongly urged that you choose the latter option.

Occasionally there are no classes available within a reasonable distance from the owner's home. Sometimes there are classes available but the tuition is too costly. Whatever the circumstances, the solution to the problem of lack of lesson availability lies within the pages of this book.

This chapter is devoted to helping you train your Border Collie at home. If the recommended procedures are followed faithfully, you may expect positive results that will prove rewarding to both you and your dog.

Whether your new charge is a puppy or a mature adult, the methods of teaching and the techniques we use in training basic behaviours are the same. After all, no dog, whether puppy or adult, likes harsh or inhumane methods. All creatures, however, respond favourably to gentle motivational methods and sincere praise and encourage-ment. Now let us get started.

HOUSEBREAKING

You can train a puppy to relieve itself wherever you choose. For example, city dwellers often train their puppies to relieve themselves in the gutter because

HOW MANY TIMES A DAY?

AGE	RELIEF TRIPS
To 14 weeks	10
14–22 weeks	8
22–32 weeks	6
Adulthood	4
(dog stops growing)	

These are estimates, of course, but they are a guide to the MINIMUM opportunities a dog should have each day to relieve itself.

large plots of grass are not readily available. Suburbanites, on the other hand, usually have gardens to accommodate their dogs' needs.

Outdoor training includes such surfaces as grass, dirt and cement. Indoor training usually means training your dog to newspaper.

When deciding on the surface and location that you will want your Border Collie to use, be sure it is going to be permanent. Training your dog to grass and then changing your mind two months later is extremely difficult for both dog and owner.

Next, choose the command you will use each and every time you want your puppy to void. 'Go hurry up' and 'Go make' are examples of commands common-ly used by dog owners.

Get in the habit of asking the puppy, 'Do you want to go hurry

Outdoor toilet training must include a dedicated area in which your dog can relieve itself.

up?' (or whatever your chosen relief command is) before you take him out. That way, when he becomes an adult, you will be able to determine if he wants to go out when you ask him. A confirmation will be signs of interest, wagging his tail, watching you intently, going to the door, etc.

PUPPY'S NEEDS

Puppy needs to relieve himself after play periods, after each

meal, after he has been sleeping and any time he indicates that he is looking for a place to urinate or defecate.

The urinary and intestinal tract muscles of very young puppies are not fully developed. Therefore, like human babies, puppies need to relieve themselves frequently.

Take your puppy out often— every hour for an eight-week-old, for example. The older the puppy, the less often he will need to relieve himself. Finally, as a mature healthy adult, he will require only three to five relief trips per day.

HOUSING

Since the types of housing and control you provide for your puppy have a direct relationship on the success of housetraining, we consider the various aspects of both before we begin training.

Bringing a new puppy home and turning him loose in your house can be compared to turning a child loose in a sports

Within that room there should be a smaller area which the puppy can call his own. A cubbyhole, a wire or fibreglass dog crate or a fenced (not boarded!) corner from which he can view the activities of his new family will be fine. The size of the area or crate is the key factor here. The area must be large enough for the puppy to lay down and stretch out as well as

Part of 'control' means limiting access to any areas in your home and garden that may be dangerous for your Border Collie.

Crate training is an effective method.

arena and telling the child that the place is all his! The sheer enormity of the place would be too much for him to handle.

Instead, offer the puppy clearly defined areas where he can play, sleep, eat and live. A room of the house where the family gathers is the most obvious choice. Puppies are social animals and need to feel a part of the pack right from the start. Hearing your voice, watching you whilst you are doing things and smelling you nearby are all positive reinforcers that he is now a member of your pack. Usually a family room, the kitchen or a nearby adjoining breakfast nook is ideal for providing safety and security for both puppy and owner.

stand up without rubbing his head on the top, yet small enough so that he cannot relieve himself at one end and sleep at the other without coming into contact with his droppings.

Dogs are, by nature, clean animals and will not remain close to their relief areas unless forced to do so. In those cases,

DID YOU KNOW?
The golden rule of dog training is simple. For each 'question' (command), there is only one correct answer (reaction). One command = one reaction. Keep practising the command until the dog reacts correctly without hesitating. Be repetitive but not monotonous. Dogs get bored just as people do!

73

If provided a properly sized crate, your Border Collie will feel comfortable and welcome the opportunity to sleep and relax in it, whether at home or on the road.

they then become dirty dogs and usually remain that way for life.

The crate or cubby should be lined with a clean towel and offer one toy, no more. Do not put food or water in the crate, as eating and drinking will activate his digestive processes and ultimately defeat your purpose as well as make the puppy very uncomfortable as he attempts to 'hold it.'

CONTROL

By control, we mean helping the puppy to create a lifestyle

DID YOU KNOW?

To a dog's way of thinking, your hands are like his mouth in terms of a defence mechanism. If you squeeze him too tightly, he might just bite you because that would be his normal response. This is not aggressive biting and, although all biting should be discouraged, you need the discipline in learning how to handle your dog.

pattern that will be compatible to that of his human pack (YOU!). Just as we guide little children to learn our way of life, we must show the puppy when it is time to play, eat, sleep, exercise and even entertain himself.

Your puppy should always sleep in his crate. He should also learn that, during times of household confusion and excessive human activity such as at breakfast when family

DID YOU KNOW?

Most of all, be consistent. Always take your dog to the same location, always use the same command, and always have him on lead when he is in his relief area, unless a fenced-in garden is available.

By following the Success Method, your puppy will be completely housetrained by the time his muscle and brain development reach maturity. Keep in mind that small breeds usually mature faster than large breeds, but all puppies should be trained by six months of age.

members are preparing for the day, he can play by himself in relative safety and comfort in his crate. Each time you leave the puppy alone, he should be crated. Puppies are chewers. They cannot tell the difference between lamp cords, television wires, shoes, table legs, etc. Chewing into a television wire,

for example, can be fatal to the puppy whilst a shorted wire can start a fire in the house.

If the puppy chews on the arm of the chair when he is alone, you will probably discipline him angrily when you get home. Thus, he makes the association that your coming home means he is going to be hit

DID YOU KNOW?

Do not carry your dog to his toilet area. Lead him there on a leash or, better yet, encourage him to follow you to the spot. If you start carrying him to his spot, you might end up doing this routine forever and your dog will have the satisfaction of having trained YOU.

DID YOU KNOW?

By providing sleeping and resting quarters that fit the dog, and offering frequent opportunities to relieve himself outside his quarters, the puppy quickly learns that the outdoors (or the newspaper if you are training him to paper) is the place to go when he needs to urinate or defecate. It also reinforces his innate desire to keep his sleeping quarters clean. This, in turn, helps develop the muscle control that will eventually produce a dog with clean living habits.

or punished. (He will not remember chewing up the chair and is incapable of making the association of the discipline with his naughty deed.)

Other times of excitement, such as family parties, etc., can be fun for the puppy providing he can view the activities from the security of his crate. He is not underfoot and he is not being fed all sorts of titbits that will probably cause him stomach distress, yet he still feels a part of the fun.

SCHEDULE

A puppy should be taken to his relief area each time he is

released from his crate, after meals, after a play session, when he first awakens in the morning (at age 8 weeks, this can mean 5 a.m.!) and whenever he indicates by circling or sniffing busily that he needs to urinate or defecate. For a puppy less than ten weeks of age, a routine of taking him out every hour is necessary. As

It's necessary to keep a schedule while travelling with your Border Collie, especially on long trips. Be sure to plan time for a few 'toilet stops.'

75

the puppy grows, he will be able to wait for longer periods of time.

Keep trips to his relief area short. Stay no more than five or six minutes and then return to the house. If he goes during that time, praise him lavishly and take him indoors immediately. If he does not, but he has an accident when you go back

It's easy to train your dog always to relieve himself in the same spot. He'll sniff around until he finds a spot he's 'visited' before.

indoors, pick him up immediately, say 'No! No!' and return to his relief area. Wait a few minutes, then return to the house again. never hit a puppy or rub his face in urine or excrement when he has an accident!

DID YOU KNOW?

Stand up straight and authoritatively when giving your dog commands. Do not issue commands when lying on the floor or lying on your back on the sofa. If you are on your hands and knees when you give a command, your dog will think you are positioning yourself to play.

DID YOU KNOW?

Your dog is actually training you at the same time you are training him. Dogs do things to get attention. They usually repeat whatever succeeds in getting your attention.

Once indoors, put the puppy in his crate until you have had time to clean up his accident. Then release him to the family area and watch him more closely than before. Chances are, his accident was a result of your not picking up his signal or waiting too long before offering him the opportunity to relieve himself. NEVER hold a grudge against the puppy for accidents.

Let the puppy learn that going outdoors means it is time to relieve himself, not play. Once trained, he will be able to play indoors and out and still differentiate between the times for play versus the times for relief.

Help him develop regular hours for naps, being alone, playing by himself and just resting, all in his crate. Encourage him to entertain himself whilst you are busy with your activities. Let him learn that having you near is comforting, but it is not your main purpose in life to provide him with undivided attention.

Each time you put a puppy in his crate tell him, 'Crate time!' (or whatever command you choose). Soon, he will run to his crate when he hears you say those words.

In the beginning of his training, do not leave him in his crate for prolonged periods of time except during the night when everyone is sleeping. Make his experience with his crate a pleasant one and, as an adult, he will love his crate and willingly stay in it for several hours. There are millions of people who go to work every day and leave their adult dogs crated whilst they are away. The dogs accept this as their lifestyle and look forward to 'crate time.'

Crate training provides safety for you, the puppy and the home. It also provides the puppy with a feeling of security, and that helps the puppy achieve self-confidence and clean habits.

Remember that one of the

DID YOU KNOW?
Dogs do not understand our language. They can be trained to react to a certain sound, at a certain volume. If you say 'No, Oliver' in a very soft pleasant voice it will not have the same meaning as 'No, Oliver!!' when you shout it as loud as you can. You should never use the dog's name during a reprimand, just the command NO!! Since dogs don't understand words, comics use dogs trained with opposite meanings. Thus, when the comic commands his dog to SIT the dog will stand up; and vice versa.

primary ingredients in housetraining your puppy is control. Regardless of your lifestyle, there will always be occasions when you will need to have a place where your dog can stay and be happy and safe. Crate

DID YOU KNOW?
The puppy should also have regular play and exercise sessions when he is with you or a family member. Exercise for a very young puppy can consist of a short walk around the house or garden. Playing can include fetching games with a large ball or a special raggy. (All puppies teethe and need soft things upon which to chew.) Remember to restrict play periods to indoors within his living area (the family room for example) until he is completely housetrained.

Once reliably housetrained, your Border Collie always should have access to water, indoors or out.

training is the answer for now and in the future.

In conclusion, a few key

77

THE SUCCESS METHOD
6 Steps to Successful Crate Training

1 Tell the puppy 'Crate time!' and place him in the crate with a small treat (a piece of cheese or half of a biscuit). Let him stay in the crate for five minutes while you are in the same room. Then release him and praise lavishly. Never release him when he is fussing. Wait until he is quiet before you let him out.

2 Repeat Step 1 several times a day.

3 The next day, place the puppy in the crate as before. Let him stay there for ten minutes. Do this several times.

4 Continue building time in five-minute increments until the puppy

stays in his crate for 30 minutes with you in the room. Always take him to his relief area after prolonged periods in his crate.

5 Now go back to Step 1 and let the puppy stay in his crate for five minutes, this time while you are out of the room.

6 Once again, build crate time in five-minute increments with you out of the room. When the puppy will stay willingly in his crate (he may even fall asleep!) for 30 minutes with you out of the room, he will be ready to stay in it for several hours at a time.

elements are really all you need for a successful house and crate training method—consistency, frequency, praise, control and supervision. By following these procedures with a normal, healthy puppy, you and the puppy will soon be past the stage of 'accidents' and ready to move on to a rewarding life together.

ROLES OF DISCIPLINE, REWARD AND PUNISHMENT
Discipline, training one to act in accordance with rules, brings order to life. It is as simple as that. Without discipline, particu-

larly in a group society, chaos reigns supreme and the group will eventually perish. Humans and canines are social animals and need some form of discipline in order to function effectively. They must procure food, protect their home base and their young and reproduce to keep the species going.

If there were no discipline in the lives of social animals, they would eventually die from starvation and/or predation by other stronger animals.

In the case of domestic canines, dogs need discipline in

Canine Development Schedule

It is important to understand how and at what age a puppy develops into adulthood. If you are a puppy owner, consult the following Canine Development Schedule to determine the stage of development your Border Collie puppy is currently experiencing. This knowledge will help you as you work with the puppy in the weeks and months ahead.

Period	Age	Characteristics
FIRST TO THIRD	**BIRTH TO SEVEN WEEKS**	Puppy needs food, sleep and warmth, and responds to simple and gentle touching. Needs mother for security and disciplining. Needs littermates for learning and interacting with other dogs. Pup learns to function within a pack and learns pack order of dominance. Begin socialising with adults and children for short periods. Begins to become aware of its environment.
FOURTH	**EIGHT TO TWELVE WEEKS**	Brain is fully developed. Needs socialising with outside world. Remove from mother and littermates. Needs to change from canine pack to human pack. Human dominance necessary. Fear period occurs between 8 and 16 weeks. Avoid fright and pain.
FIFTH	**THIRTEEN TO SIXTEEN WEEKS**	Training and formal obedience should begin. Less association with other dogs, more with people, places, situations. Period will pass easily if you remember this is pup's change-to-adolescence time. Be firm and fair. Flight instinct prominent. Permissiveness and over-disciplining can do permanent damage. Praise for good behaviour.
JUVENILE	**FOUR TO EIGHT MONTHS**	Another fear period about 7 to 8 months of age. It passes quickly, but be cautious of fright and pain. Sexual maturity reached. Dominant traits established. Dog should understand sit, down, come and stay by now.

NOTE: THESE ARE APPROXIMATE TIME FRAMES. ALLOW FOR INDIVIDUAL DIFFERENCES IN PUPPIES.

Border Collies love to work, and these instincts translate into a highly trainable pet dog that is eager to please his master.

DID YOU KNOW?

Never line your pup's sleeping area with newspaper. Puppy litters are usually raised on newspaper and, once in your home, the puppy will immediately associate newspaper with voiding. Never put newspaper on any floor while housetraining, as this will only confuse the puppy. If you are paper-training him, use paper in his designated relief area ONLY. Finally, restrict water intake after evening meals. Offer a few licks at a time—never let a young puppy gulp water after meals.

their lives in order to understand how their pack (you and other family members) functions and how they must act in order to survive.

A large humane society in a highly populated area recently surveyed dog owners regarding their satisfaction with their relationships with their dogs. People who had trained their dogs were 75% more satisfied with their pets than those who had never trained their dogs.

Dr. Edward Thorndike, a psychologist, established *Thorndike's Theory of Learning*, which states that a behaviour that results in a pleasant event tends to be repeated. A behaviour that results in an unpleasant event tends not to be repeated. It is this theory on which training methods are based today. For example, if you manipulate a dog to perform a specific behaviour and reward him for doing it, he is likely to do it again because he enjoyed the end result.

Occasionally, punishment, a penalty inflicted for an offence, is necessary. The best type of punishment often comes from an outside source. For example, a child is told not to touch the stove because he may get burned. He disobeys and touches the stove. In doing so, he receives a burn. From

A Border Collie will truly be a 'reflection' of his owner and the training that the dog receives.

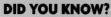

DID YOU KNOW?

Practice Makes Perfect!
• Have training lessons with your dog every day in several short segments—three to five times a day for a few minutes at a time is ideal.
• Do not have long practice sessions. The dog will become easily bored.
• Never practice when you are tired, ill, worried or in an otherwise negative mood. This will transmit to the dog and may have an adverse effect on its performance.

Think fun, short and above all POSITIVE! End each session on a high note, rather than a failed exercise, and make sure to give a lot of praise. Enjoy the training and help your dog enjoy it, too.

that time on, he respects the heat of the stove and avoids contact with it. Therefore, a behaviour that results in an unpleasant event tends not to be repeated.

A good example of a dog learning the hard way is the dog who chases the house cat. He is told many times to leave the cat alone, yet he persists in teasing the cat. Then, one day he begins chasing the cat but the cat turns and swipes a claw across the dog's face, leaving him with a painful gash on his nose. The final result is that the dog stops chasing the cat.

81

CHOOSE THE PROPER COLLAR

The buckle collar is the standard collar used for everyday purpose. Be sure that you adjust the buckle on growing puppies. Check it every day. It can become too tight overnight! These collars can be made of leather or nylon. Attach your dog's identification tags to this collar.

The choke chain is the usual collar recommended for training. It is constructed of highly polished steel so that it slides easily through the stainless steel loop. The idea is that the dog controls the pressure around its neck and he will stop pulling if the collar becomes uncomfortable. Never leave a choke collar on your dog when not training.

The halter is for a trained dog that has to be restrained to prevent running away, chasing a cat and the like. Considered the most humane of all collars, it is frequently used on smaller dogs for which collars are not comfortable.

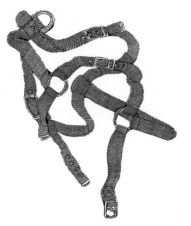

TRAINING EQUIPMENT

COLLAR

A simple buckle collar is fine for most dogs. One who pulls mightily on the leash may require a chain choker collar. Only in the most severe cases of a dog being totally out of control is the use of a prong or pinch collar recommended. These collars should only be used by owners with experience in the proper use of such equipment. In some areas, such as the United Kingdom, these types of collars are not allowed.

LEAD

A 1- to 2-metre lead is recommended, preferably made of leather, nylon or heavy cloth. A chain lead is not recommended, as many dog owners find that the chain cuts into their hands and that frequently switching the lead back and forth between their hands is painful.

TREATS

Have a bag of treats on hand. Something nutritious and easy to swallow works best. Use a soft treat, a chunk of cheese or a piece of cooked chicken rather than a dry biscuit. By the time the dog gets done chewing a dry treat, he will forget why he is being rewarded in the first place! Using food rewards will not teach a dog to beg at the table—the only way to teach a dog to beg at the table is

within a foot of the dog. Do not go directly to him, but stop about a foot short of him and hold out the treat as you ask, 'School?' He will see you approaching with a treat in your hand and most likely begin walking toward you. As you meet, give him the treat and praise again.

The third time, ask the question, have a treat in your hand and walk only a short distance toward the dog so that he must walk almost all the way to you.

Lightweight buckle collars can either be leather or nylon.

to give him food from the table. In training, rewarding the dog with a food treat will help him associate praise and the treats with learning new behaviours that obviously please his owner.

TRAINING BEGINS: ASK THE DOG A QUESTION

In order to teach your dog anything, you must first get his attention. After all, he cannot learn anything if he is looking away from you with his mind on something else.

To get his attention, ask him, 'School?' and immediately walk over to him and give him a treat as you tell him 'Good dog.' Wait a minute or two and repeat the routine, this time with a treat in your hand as you approach

There are many kinds of leads. Discuss your choices with your local pet shop. These pups are being exposed to their leads as a group project!

83

Once your Border Collie is trained to sit, you can progress to the sit/stay. This is best taught by gradually increasing the length of time and distance from the dog.

As he reaches you, give him the treat and praise again.

By this time, the dog will probably be getting the idea that if he pays attention to you, especially when you ask that question, it will pay off in treats and fun activities for him. In other words, he learns that 'school' means doing fun things with you that result in treats and positive attention for him.

Remember that the dog does not understand your verbal language, he only recognises sounds. Your question translates to a series of sounds for him, and those sounds become the signal to go to you and pay attention; if he does, he will get to interact with you plus receive treats and praise.

THE BASIC COMMANDS
TEACHING SIT

Now that you have the dog's attention, attach his lead and hold it in your left hand and a food treat in your right. Place your food hand at the dog's nose and let him lick the treat but not take it from you. Say 'Sit' and slowly raise your food hand from in front of the dog's nose up over his head so that he is looking at the ceiling. As he bends his head upward, he will have to bend his knees to maintain his balance. As he bends his knees, he will assume a sit position. At that point, release the food treat and praise lavishly with comments such as 'Good dog! Good sit!', etc. Remember to always praise enthusiastically, because dogs relish verbal praise from their owners and feel so proud of themselves whenever they accomplish a behaviour.

Food treats, training rewards or bribes, regardless of what you call them, should not become a way of life. Your dog must be weaned off them sooner or later.

You will not use food forever in getting the dog to obey your commands. Food is only used to teach new behaviours, and once the dog knows what you want when you give a specific command, you will wean him off of the food treats but still maintain the verbal praise. After

Your Border Collie is what you make of him. He can be a trained pet or an ill-behaved nuisance.

all, you will always have your voice with you, and there will be many times when you have no food rewards but expect the dog to obey.

DID YOU KNOW?

Occasionally, a dog and owner who have not attended formal classes have been able to earn entry-level titles by obtaining competition rules and regulations from a local kennel club and practising on their own to a degree of perfection. Obtaining the higher level titles, however, almost always requires extensive training under the tutelage of experienced instructors. In addition, the more difficult levels require more specialised equipment whereas the lower levels do not.

TEACHING DOWN

Teaching the down exercise is easy when you understand how the dog perceives the down position, and it is very difficult when you do not. Dogs perceive the down position as a submissive one, therefore teaching the down exercise using a forceful method can sometimes make the

Border Collies are easily trained to sit. Gently assisting the dog into position is an acceptable method. Keep in mind that successful performances should be rewarded with verbal praise.

Now place the food hand at the dog's nose, say 'Down' very softly (almost a whisper), and slowly lower the food hand to the dog's front feet. When the food hand reaches the floor, begin moving it forward along the floor in front of the dog. Keep talking softly to the dog, saying things like, 'Do you want this treat? You can do this, good dog.' Your reassuring tone of voice will help calm the dog as he tries to follow the food hand in order to get the treat.

When the dog's elbows touch the floor, release the food and praise softly. Try to get the dog to maintain that down position for several seconds before you let him sit up again. The goal here is to get the dog to settle down and not feel threatened in the down position.

dog develop such a fear of the down that he either runs away when you say 'Down' or he attempts to bite the person who tries to force him down.

Have the dog sit close alongside your left leg, facing in the same direction as you are. Hold the lead in your left hand and a food treat in your right. Now place your left hand lightly on the top of the dog's shoulders where they meet above the spinal cord. Do not push down on the dog's shoulders; simply rest your left hand there so you can guide the dog to lie down close to your left leg rather than to swing away from your side when he drops.

DID YOU KNOW?

A basic obedience beginner's class usually lasts for six to eight weeks. Dog and owner attend an hour-long lesson once a week and practice for a few minutes, several times a day, each day at home. If done properly, the whole procedure will result in a well-mannered dog and an owner who delights in living with a pet that is eager to please and enjoys doing things with his owner.

TEACHING STAY

It is easy to teach the dog to stay in either a sit or a down position. Again, we use food and praise during the teaching process as we help the dog to understand exactly what it is that we are expecting him to do.

To teach the sit/stay, start with the dog sitting on your left side as before and hold the lead in your left hand. Have a food treat in your right hand and place your food hand at the dog's nose. Say 'Stay' and step out on your right foot to stand directly in front of the dog, toe to toe, as he licks and nibbles the treat. Be sure to keep his head facing upward to maintain the sit position. Count to five and then swing around to stand next to the dog again with him on your left. As soon as you get back to the original position, release the food and praise lavishly.

To teach the down/stay, do the down as previously described. As soon as the dog lies down, say 'Stay' and step out on your right foot just as you did in the sit/stay. Count to five and then return to stand beside the dog

> **DID YOU KNOW?**
>
> A dog in jeopardy never lies down. He stays alert on his feet because instinct tells him that he may have to run away or fight for his survival. Therefore, if a dog feels threatened or anxious, he will not lie down. Consequently, it is important to have the dog calm and relaxed as he learns the down exercise.

with him on your left side. Release the treat and praise as always.

Within a week or ten days, you can begin to add a bit of distance between you and your dog when you leave him. When you do, use your left hand open with the palm facing the dog as a stay signal, much the same as the hand signal a police officer uses

Dogs perceive the down position as one of submission. Do not attempt to push the dog into the down position, as he can become fearful of this exercise.

Advanced training often uses hand signals, either in place of or along with verbal commands.

TEACHING COME

If you make teaching 'come' a fun experience, you should never have a 'student' that does not love the game or that fails to come when called. The secret, it seems, is never to teach the word 'come.'

At times when an owner most wants his dog to come when called, the owner is likely upset or anxious and he allows these feelings to come through in the tone of his voice when he calls his dog. Hearing that desperation in his owner's voice, the dog fears the results of going to him and therefore either disobeys outright or runs in the opposite direction. The secret, therefore, is to teach the dog a game and, when you want him to come to you, simply play the game. It is practically a no-fail solution!

To begin, have several members of your family take a few food treats and each go into a different room in the house.

to stop traffic at an intersection. Hold the food treat in your right hand as before, but this time the food is not touching the dog's nose. He will watch the food hand and quickly learn that he is going to get that treat as soon as you return to his side.

When you can stand 1 metre away from your dog for 30 seconds, you can then begin building time and distance in both stays. Eventually, the dog can be expected to remain in the stay position for prolonged periods of time until you return to him or call him to you. Always praise lavishly when he stays.

DID YOU KNOW?

Taking your dog to an obedience school may be the best investment in time and money you can ever make. You will enjoy the benefits for the lifetime of your dog and you will have the opportunity to meet people with your similar expectations for companion dogs.

Take turns calling the dog, and each person should celebrate the dog's finding him with a treat and lots of happy praise. When a person calls the dog, he is actually inviting the dog to find him and get a treat as a reward for 'winning.'

A few turns of the 'Where are you?' game and the dog will figure out that everyone is playing the game and that each person has a big celebration awaiting his success at locating them. Once he learns to love the game, simply calling out 'Where are you?' will bring him running from wherever he is when he hears that all-important question.

The come command is recognised as one of the most important things to teach a dog, but there are trainers who work with thousands of dogs and never teach the actual word 'Come.' Yet these dogs will race to respond to a person who uses the dog's name followed by 'Where are you?' For example, a woman has a 12-year-old companion dog who went blind, but who never fails to locate her owner when asked, 'Where are you?'

Children particularly love to play this game with their dogs. Children can hide in smaller places like a shower or bathtub, behind a bed or under a table. The dog needs to work a little bit harder to find these hiding

DID YOU KNOW?
When calling the dog, do not say 'Come.' Say things like, 'Rover, where are you? See if you can find me! I have a cookie for you!' Keep up a constant line of chatter with coaxing sounds and frequent questions such as, 'Where are you?' The dog will learn to follow the sound of your voice to locate you and receive his reward.

places, but when he does he loves to celebrate with a treat and a tussle with a favourite youngster.

TEACHING HEEL
Heeling means that the dog walks beside the owner without pulling. It takes time and patience on the owner's part to succeed at teaching the dog that he (the owner) will not proceed

'Come' must be a win-win situation. Let the dog feel like he's a winner because he comes to you.

unless the dog is walking calmly beside him. Pulling out ahead on the lead is definitely not acceptable.

Begin with holding the lead in your left hand as the dog sits

89

Teaching your dog to heel requires that he walk alongside you, at your pace, without pulling or jerking the lead. Show dogs exhibit the heel expertly.

beside your left leg. Move the loop end of the lead to your right hand but keep your left hand short on the lead so it keeps the dog in close next to you.

Say 'Heel' and step forward on your left foot. Keep the dog close to you and take three steps. Stop and have the dog sit next to you in what we now call the 'heel position.' Praise verbally, but do not touch the dog. Hesitate a moment and begin again with 'Heel,' taking three steps and stopping, at which point the dog is told to sit again.

Your goal here is to have the dog walk those three steps without pulling on the lead. When he will walk calmly beside

you for three steps without pulling, increase the number of steps you take to five. When he will walk politely beside you whilst you take five steps, you can increase the length of your walk to ten steps. Keep increasing the length of your stroll until the dog will walk quietly beside you without pulling as long as you want him to heel. When you stop heeling, indicate to the dog that the exercise is over by verbally praising as you pet him and say 'OK, good dog.' The 'OK' is used as a release word meaning that the exercise is finished and the dog is free to relax.

If you are dealing with a dog who insists on pulling you around, simply 'put on your brakes' and stand your ground until the dog realises that the two of you are not going anywhere until he is beside you and moving at your pace, not his. It may take some time just standing there to convince the dog that you are the leader and you will be the one to decide on the direction and speed of your travel.

Each time the dog looks up at you or slows down to give a slack lead between the two of you, quietly praise him and say, 'Good heel. Good dog.' Eventually, the dog will begin to respond and within a few days he will be walking politely

DID YOU KNOW?
Teach your dog to HEEL in an enclosed area. Once you think the dog will obey reliably and you want to attempt advanced obedience exercises such as off-lead heeling, test him in a fenced in area so he cannot run away.

DID YOU KNOW?

If you begin teaching the heel by taking long walks and letting the dog pull you along, he misinterprets this action as an acceptable form of taking a walk. When you pull back on the lead to counteract his pulling, he reads that tug as a signal to pull even harder!

Training lessons create a wonderful bond between you and your dog. Thus, a well-trained Border Collie is not only a better behaved pet but also a more enjoyable companion.

beside you without pulling on the lead. At first, the training sessions should be kept short and very positive; soon the dog will be able to walk nicely with you for increasingly longer distances. Remember also to give the dog free time and the opportunity to run and play when you are done with heel practice.

WEANING OFF FOOD IN TRAINING

Food is used in training new behaviours. Once the dog understands what behaviour goes with a specific command, it is time to start weaning him off the food treats. At first, give a treat after each exercise. Then, start to give a treat only after every other exercise. Mix up the times when you offer a food reward and the times when you only offer praise so that the dog will never know when he is going to receive both food and praise and when he is going to receive only praise. This is called a variable ratio reward system and it proves successful because there is always the chance that the owner will produce a treat, so the dog never stops trying for that reward. No matter what, ALWAYS give verbal praise.

OBEDIENCE CLASSES

As previously discussed, it is a good idea to enrol in an

DID YOU KNOW?

If you are walking your dog and he suddenly stops and looks straight into your eyes, ignore him. Pull the leash and lead him into the direction you want to walk.

obedience class if one is available in your area. Many areas have dog clubs that offer basic obedience training as well as preparatory classes for obedience competition. There are also local dog trainers who offer similar classes.

At obedience trials, dogs can earn titles at various levels of competition. The beginning levels of competition include basic behaviours such as sit, down, heel, etc. The more advanced levels of competition include jumping, retrieving, scent discrimination and signal work. The advanced levels require a dog and owner to put a lot of time and effort into their training and the titles that can be earned at these levels of competition are very prestigious.

OTHER ACTIVITIES FOR LIFE
Whether a dog is trained in the structured environment of a class or alone with his owner at home, there are many activities that can bring fun and rewards to both owner and dog once they have mastered basic control.

Teaching the dog to help out around the home, in the garden or on the farm provides great satisfaction to both dog and owner. In addition, the dog's help makes life a little easier for

Obedience classes are great experiences for your dog to socialise with other canines. Owners also profit from talking to other dog people to discuss the rewards and challenges of dog training.

his owner and raises his stature as a valued companion to his family. It helps give the dog a purpose by occupying his mind and providing an outlet for his energy.

Backpacking is an exciting and healthful activity that the dog can be taught without assistance from more than his owner. The exercise of walking and climbing is good for man and dog alike, and the bond that they develop together is priceless.

If you are interested in participating in organised competition with your Border Collie, there are activities other than obedience in which you and your dog can become involved. Agility is a popular and fun sport where dogs run through an obstacle course that includes various jumps, tunnels and other exercises to test the dog's speed and coordination. The owners run through the course beside their dogs to give commands and to guide them through the course.

Tossing a flying disc is an excellent pastime for the Border Collie. It's also an ideal outlet for the owner who does not want to do as much running as his dog.

Although competitive, the focus is on fun—it's fun to do, fun to watch, and great exercise. Border Collies prove exceptional at agility trials, just as they do obedience trials.

Of course, the true Border Collie pastime is sheepdog trials, which are the most popular amongst Border Collie enthusiasts. It is exciting and rewarding to watch the talented and swift Border Collie work in its born-for capacity.

Sheepdog trials give the Border Collie an opportunity to use its natural herding instincts. These trials are great fun for dog, handler and audience alike.

93

MEDICAL PROBLEMS MOST FREQUENTLY SEEN IN BORDER COLLIES

HIP DYSPLASIA (HD)

Hip dysplasia (HD) is manifested by the malformation of the hip joint and its not properly fitting into the socket. Studies indicate that the disease is 70% hereditary and 30% environmental. In Border Collies, the environmental factors include oversupplementation and feeding as well as strenuous play for puppies. Young Border Collies should never be started on work before the age of one year. Compared to some other breeds, the Border Collie suffers from a relatively high incidence of HD, with only over 50-percent 'normal' and about 7-percent 'moderate' to 'severe.'

Focal/Multifocal Acquired Retinopathy (FMAR) causes retinal lesions in the breed, as it does in many performance dogs such as Greyhounds, Siberian Huskies, and other herding dogs. FMAR may be inherited, but it has not been conclusively determined. It is often confused with PRA or dismissed as scars from distemper or worm infestation. It is more often seen in males and has become alarmingly common in Border Collies.

Ceroid Lipofuscinosis (CL) is an inherited disease that affects the Border Collie. CL is characterised by abnormal behaviour, blindness and mental vagueness. Brain atrophy accompanied by high accumulation of ceroid bodies in nerve tissues describes the disease.

Central Progressive Retinal Atrophy (CPRA), once widespread in the breed, appears to be disappearing in European and British Border Collies. The disease is hereditary but seems to be preventable through diet and certain environmental factors. CPRA affects the retinal pigment epithelium, a layer of cells that nourish the retinal nerve cells.

Collie Eye Anomaly (CEA) affects the correct formation of the eye in herding breeds. In the Border Collie, the disease resembles CEA in Rough and Smooth Collies and is likely inherited as an autosomal recessive trait. In the worst cases, blindness occurs preceded by retinal detachments and haemorrhages.

Progressive Retinal Atrophy (PRA) is a blinding, hereditary disorder seen in most purebred dogs. Early signs of PRA include nightblindness, inability to adjust vision in dim light and eventual failing day vision. The rods and later the cones are affected, eventually causing blindness. Border Collies most often develop PRA at two years or older.

Epilepsy is a seizure disorder that has been found in many lines of Border Collies. Since there are no tests for epilepsy and the disorder can occur later in life, it is difficult to breed epilepsy out of a line. Breeders are strongly discouraged from breeding a known epileptic dog.

Border Collie

Dogs suffer many of the same physical illnesses as people. They might even share many of the same psychological problems. Since people usually know more about human diseases than canine maladies, many of the terms used in this chapter will be familiar but not necessarily those used by veterinary surgeons. We will use the term *x-ray*, instead of the more acceptable term *radiograph*. We will also use the familiar term *symptoms* even though dogs don't have *symptoms*, which are verbal descriptions of the patient's feelings; dogs have *clinical signs*. Since dogs can't speak, we have to look for clinical signs...but we still use the term symptoms in this book.

As a general rule, medicine is practised. That term is not arbitrary. Medicine is a constantly changing art as we learn more and more about genetics, electronic aids (like CAT scans) and daily laboratory advances. There are many dog maladies, like canine hip dysplasia, which are not universally treated in the same manner. Some veterinary surgeons opt for surgery more often than others do.

SELECTING A VETERINARY SURGEON

Your selection of a veterinary surgeon should not be based upon personality (as most are) but upon their convenience to your home. You want a doctor who is close because you might have emergencies or need to make multiple visits for treatments. You want a doctor who has services that you might require such as a boarding kennel and grooming facilities, as well as sophisticated pet supplies

Dogs do not sweat. By panting, their tongues are used to cool their blood.

and a good reputation for ability and responsiveness. There is nothing more frustrating than having to wait a day or more to get a response from your veterinary surgeon.

All veterinary surgeons are licensed and their diplomas and/or certificates should be displayed in their waiting rooms. There are, however, many veterinary specialties that usually

95

All veterinary surgeons are licensed and all have been taught to read x-rays, but there are specialists called veterinary radiologists who are consulted for the fine details of x-ray interpretations.

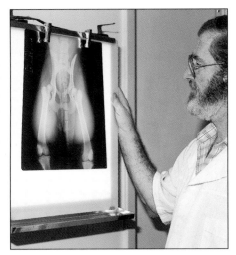

require further studies and internships. There are specialists in heart problems (veterinary cardiologists), skin problems (veterinary dermatologists), teeth and gum problems (veterinary dentists), eye problems (veterinary ophthalmologists), X-rays (veterinary radiologists), and surgeons who have specialties in bones, muscles or other organs. Most veterinary surgeons do routine surgery such as neutering, stitching up wounds and docking tails for those breeds in which such is required for show purposes. When the problem affecting your dog is serious, it is not unusual or impudent to get another medical opinion. You might also want to compare costs amongst several veterinary surgeons. Sophisticated health care and veterinary services can be very costly. Don't be bashful about discussing these costs with your veterinary surgeon or his (her) staff. It is not infrequent that important decisions are based upon financial considerations.

PREVENTATIVE MEDICINE

It is much easier, less costly and more effective to practise preventative medicine than to fight bouts of illness and disease. Properly bred puppies come from parents that were selected based upon their genetic disease profiles. Their mothers should have been vaccinated, free of all internal and external parasites, and properly nourished. For these reasons, a visit to the veterinary surgeon who cared for the dam (mother) is recommended. The dam can pass on disease resistance to her puppies, which can last for eight to ten weeks. She can also pass on parasites and many infections. That's why you should visit the veterinary surgeon who cared for the dam.

DID YOU KNOW?

Your veterinary surgeon will probably recommend that your puppy be vaccinated before you take him outside. There are airborne diseases, parasite eggs in the grass and unexpected visits from other dogs that might be dangerous to your puppy's health.

WEANING TO FIVE MONTHS OLD

Puppies should be weaned by the time they are about two months old. A puppy that remains for at least eight weeks with its mother and litter mates usually adapts better to other dogs and people later in its life.

In every case, you should have your newly acquired puppy examined by a veterinary surgeon immediately. Vaccination programmes usually begin when the puppy is very young.

The puppy will have its teeth examined and have its skeletal conformation and general health checked prior to certification by the veterinary surgeon. Many puppies have problems with their kneecaps, eye cataracts and other eye problems, heart murmurs and undescended testicles. They may also have personality problems and your veterinary surgeon might have training in temperament evaluation.

VACCINATION SCHEDULING

Most vaccinations are given by injection and should only be done by a veterinary surgeon. Both he and you should keep a record of the date of the injection, the identification of the vaccine and the amount given. The first vaccinations should start when the puppy is 6–8 weeks old, the second when it is 10–12 weeks of age and the third when it is 14–16 weeks of age. Vaccinations should

DID YOU KNOW?

A dental examination is in order when the dog is between six months and one year of age so any permanent teeth that have erupted incorrectly can be corrected. It is important to begin a brushing routine, preferably using a two-sided brushing technique, whereby both sides of the tooth are brushed at the same time. Durable nylon and

safe edible chews should be a part of your puppy's arsenal for good health, good teeth and pleasant breath. The vast majority of dogs three to four years old and older has diseases of their gums from lack of dental attention. Using the various types of dental chews can be very effective in controlling dental plaque.

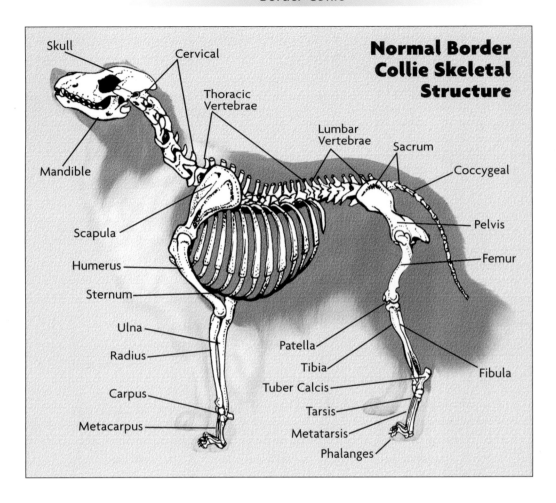

Normal Border Collie Skeletal Structure

Skull
Cervical
Thoracic Vertebrae
Lumbar Vertebrae
Sacrum
Coccygeal
Mandible
Pelvis
Femur
Scapula
Humerus
Sternum
Ulna
Radius
Patella
Tibia
Tuber Calcis
Fibula
Carpus
Tarsis
Metacarpus
Metatarsis
Phalanges

never be given without a 15-day lapse between injections. Most vaccinations immunise your puppy against viruses.

The usual vaccines contain immunising doses of several different viruses such as distemper, parvovirus, parainfluenza and hepatitis. There are other vaccines available when the puppy is at risk. You should rely upon profes-

DID YOU KNOW?

Vaccines do not work all the time. Sometimes dogs are allergic to them and many times the antibodies, which are supposed to be stimulated by the vaccine, just are not produced. You should keep your dog in the veterinary clinic for an hour after it is vaccinated to be sure there are no allergic reactions.

sional advice. This is especially true for the booster-shot programme. Most vaccination programmes require a booster when the puppy is a year old and once a year thereafter. In some cases, circumstances may require more frequent immunisations. Canine cough, more formally known as tracheobronchitis, is treated with a vaccine that is sprayed into the dog's nostrils.

The effectiveness of a parvovirus vaccination programme can be tested using the parvovirus antibody titer to be certain that the vaccinations are

DID YOU KNOW?

Anaesthetising a dog can be dangerous but especially so with the Border Collie. Be certain that your veterinary surgeon is aware that the breed seems to be overly sensitive to thiobarbituates, such as Surital, which requires that the body fat be metabolised. The Border Collie, particularly in lean working condition, has a very low percentage of body fat.

HEALTH AND VACCINATION SCHEDULE

AGE IN WEEKS:	3RD	6TH	8TH	10TH	12TH	14TH	16TH	20-24TH
Worm Control	✔	✔	✔	✔	✔	✔	✔	✔
Neutering								✔
Heartworm*		✔						✔
Parvovirus		✔		✔		✔		✔
Distemper			✔		✔		✔	
Hepatitis			✔		✔		✔	
Leptospirosis		✔		✔		✔		
Parainfluenza		✔		✔		✔		
Dental Examination			✔					✔
Complete Physical			✔					✔
Temperament Testing			✔					
Coronavirus					✔			
Canine Cough		✔						
Hip Dysplasia							✔	
Rabies*								✔

Vaccinations are not instantly effective. It takes about two weeks for the dog's immune system to develop antibodies. Most vaccinations require annual booster shots. Your veterinary surgeon should guide you in this regard.
*Not applicable in the United Kingdom

protective. Your veterinary surgeon will explain and manage all of these details.

FIVE MONTHS TO ONE YEAR OF AGE

By the time your puppy is five months old, he should have completed his vaccination programme. During his physical examination he should be evaluated for the common hip dysplasia and other diseases of the joints. There are tests to assist in the prediction of these problems. Other tests can be run to assess the effectiveness of the vaccination programme.

Unless you intend to breed or show your dog, neutering the puppy at six months of age is recommended. Discuss this with your veterinary surgeon.

Most professionals advise neutering the puppy. Neutering has proven to be extremely beneficial to both male and female puppies. Besides eliminating the possibility of pregnancy, it inhibits (but does not prevent) breast cancer in bitches and prostate cancer in male dogs.

DOGS OLDER THAN ONE YEAR

Continue to visit the veterinary surgeon at least once a year. There is no such disease as old age, but bodily functions do change with age. The eyes and ears are no longer as efficient. Liver, kidney and intestinal functions often decline. Proper dietary changes,

DO YOU KNOW ABOUT HIP DYSPLASIA?

Hip dysplasia is a fairly common condition found in Border Collies, as well as other breeds. When a dog has hip dysplasia, its hind leg has an incorrectly formed hip joint. By constant use of the hip joint, it becomes more and more loose, wears abnormally and may become arthritic.

Hip dysplasia can only be confirmed with an X-ray, but certain symptoms may indicate a problem. Your Border Collie may have a hip dysplasia problem if it walks in a peculiar manner, hops instead of smoothly running, uses his hinds legs in unison (to keep the pressure off the weak joint), has trouble getting up from a prone position and always sits with both legs together on one side of its body.

As the dog matures, it may adapt well to life with a bad hip, but in a few years the arthritis develops and many Border Collies with hip dysplasia become cripples.

Hip dysplasia is considered an inherited disease and can usually be diagnosed when the dog is three to nine months old. Some experts claim that a special diet might help your puppy outgrow the bad hip, but the usual treatments are surgical: the removal of the pectineus muscle, the removal of the round part of the femur, reconstructing the pelvis and replacing the hip with an artificial one. All of these surgical interventions are expensive, but they are usually very successful. Follow the advice of your veterinary surgeon.

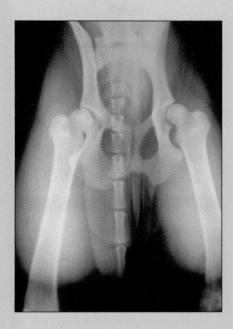

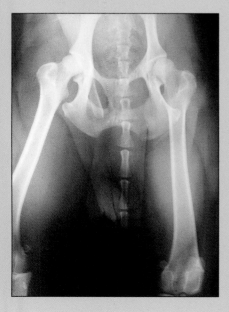

Compare the two hip joints and you'll understand dysplasia. Hip dysplasia is a badly worn hip joint caused by improper fit of the bone into the socket.

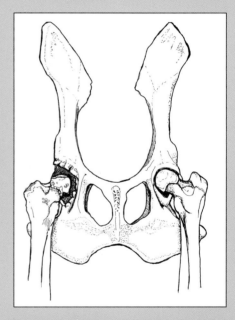

The healthy hip joint on the right and the unhealthy hip joint on the left.

Hip dysplasia can only be positively diagnosed by x-ray. Border Collies manifest the problem when they are between four and nine months of age, the so-called fast growth period.

Genetic predisposition to hip dysplasia and skin problems can easily be passed from mother to puppy.

almost as sensitive as human skin and both suffer almost the same ailments (though the occurrence of acne in dogs is rare!) For this reason, veterinary dermatology has developed into a specialty practised by many veterinary surgeons.

Since many skin problems have visual symptoms that are almost identical, it requires the skill of an experienced veterinary dermatologist to identify and cure many of the more severe skin disorders. Pet shops sell many treatments for skin problems but most of the treatments are direct-ed at symptoms and not the underlying problem(s). If your dog is suffering from a skin disorder,

recommended by your veterinary surgeon, can make life more pleasant for the ageing Border Collie and you.

SKIN PROBLEMS IN BORDER COLLIES

Veterinary surgeons are consulted by dog owners for skin problems more than any other group of diseases or maladies. Dogs' skin is

Disease	What is it?	What causes it?	Symptoms
Leptospirosis	Severe disease that affects the internal organs; can be spread to people.	A bacterium, which is often carried by rodents, that enters through mucous membranes and spreads quickly throughout the body.	Range from fever, vomiting and loss of appetite in less severe cases to shock, irreversible kidney damage and possibly death in most severe cases.
Rabies	Potentially deadly virus that infects warm-blooded mammals. Not seen in United Kingdom.	Bite from a carrier of the virus, mainly wild animals.	1st stage: dog exhibits change in behaviour, fear. 2nd stage: dog's behaviour becomes more aggressive. 3rd stage: loss of coordination, trouble with bodily functions.
Parvovirus	Highly contagious virus, potentially deadly.	Ingestion of the virus, which is usually spread through the faeces of infected dogs.	Most common: severe diarrhoea. Also vomiting, fatigue, lack of appetite.
Kennel cough	Contagious respiratory infection.	Combination of types of bacteria and virus. Most common: *Bordetella bronchiseptica* bacteria and parainfluenza virus.	Chronic cough.
Distemper	Disease primarily affecting respiratory and nervous system.	Virus that is related to the human measles virus.	Mild symptoms such as fever, lack of appetite and mucous secretion progress to evidence of brain damage, 'hard pad.'
Hepatitis	Virus primarily affecting the liver.	Canine adenovirus type I (CAV-1). Enters system when dog breathes in particles.	Lesser symptoms include listlessness, diarrhoea, vomiting. More severe symptoms include 'blue-eye' (clumps of virus in eye).
Coronavirus	Virus resulting in digestive problems.	Virus is spread through infected dog's faeces.	Stomach upset evidenced by lack of appetite, vomiting, diarrhoea.

you should seek professional assistance as quickly as possible. As with all diseases, the earlier a problem is identified and treated, the more successful is the cure.

ACRAL LICK GRANULOMA

Border Collies and other dogs of about the same size have a very poorly understood syndrome called acral lick. The manifestation of the problem is the dog's tireless attack at a specific area of the body, almost always the legs. They lick so intensively that they remove the hair and skin leaving an ugly, large wound. There is no absolute cure, but corticosteroids are the most common treatment.

DID YOU KNOW?
Owners can do their part in preventing the onset of hip dysplasia. Never overfeed your Border Collie puppy. Keep the puppy about 20-percent under-weight: you should still be able to feel the athletic dog's ribs and vertebrae. Overweight is never acceptable on a Border Collie. Excess poundage on a working dog can also put the dog at risk of heart attack or exhaustion. Never begin working or seriously training a puppy before it is one year of age. Such stress can also instigate the onset of HD.

INHERITED SKIN PROBLEMS

Many skin disorders are inherited and some are fatal. For example, Acrodermatitis is an inherited disease that is transmitted by both parents. The parents, who appear (phenotypically) normal, have a recessive gene for acrodermatitis, meaning that they carry, but are not affected by the disease.

Acrodermatitis is just one example of how difficult it is to prevent congenital dog diseases. The cost and skills required to ascertain whether two dogs should be mated are too high even though puppies with acrodermatitis rarely reach two years of age.

Other inherited skin problems are usually not as fatal as acrodermatitis. All inherited diseases must be diagnosed and treated by a veterinary specialist. There are active programmes being undertaken by many veteri-nary pharmaceutical manufactur-ers to solve most, if not all, of the common skin problems of dogs.

Acral lick syndrome is manifested by a large, raw lick granuloma usually found on the dog's front leg. Its cause is unknown, though boredom often leads to this problem in Border Collies.

DID YOU KNOW?

There is a 25% chance of a puppy getting this fatal gene combination from two parents with recessive genes for acrodermatitis:

AA= NORMAL, HEALTHY
aa= FATAL
Aa= RECESSIVE, NORMAL APPEARING

If the female parent has an Aa gene and the male parent has an Aa gene, the chances are one in four that the puppy will have the fatal genetic combination aa.

	Dam		♀
	A	a	
A	AA	Aa	
a	Aa	aa	
♂			

itching from parasite bites is probably due to the saliva injected into the site when the parasite sucks the dog's blood.

AUTO-IMMUNE SKIN CONDITIONS

Auto-immune skin conditions are commonly referred to as being allergic to yourself, whilst allergies are usually inflammatory reactions to an outside stimulus. Auto-immune diseases cause serious damage to the tissues that are involved.

The best known auto-immune disease is lupus, which affects people as well as dogs. The symptoms are variable and may affect the kidneys, bones, blood chemistry and skin. It can be fatal to both dogs and humans, though it is not thought to be transmissible. It is usually successfully treated with cortisone, prednisone or similar corticosteroid, but extensive use of these drugs can have harmful side effects.

PARASITE BITES

Many of us are allergic to mosquito bites. The bites itch, erupt and may even become infected. Dogs have the same reaction to fleas, ticks and/or mites. When you feel the prick of the mosquito as it bites you, you have a chance to kill it with your hand. Unfortunately, when our dog is bitten by a flea, tick or mite, it can only scratch it away or bite it. By the time the dog has been bitten, the parasite has done some of its damage. It may also have laid eggs to cause further problems in the near future. The

AIRBORNE ALLERGIES

Another interesting allergy is pollen allergy. Humans have hay

DID YOU KNOW?

Cases of hyperactive adrenal glands (Cushing's disease) have been traced to the drinking of highly chlorinated water. Aerate or age your dog's drinking water before offering it.

fever, rose fever and other fevers with which they suffer during the pollinating season. Many dogs suffer the same allergies. When the pollen count is high, your dog might suffer but don't expect them to sneeze and have runny noses like humans. Dogs react to pollen allergies the same way they react to fleas—they scratch and bite themselves. Border Collies are very susceptible to airborne pollen allergies.

Dogs, like humans, can be tested for allergens. Discuss the testing with your veterinary dermatologist.

FOOD PROBLEMS
FOOD ALLERGIES
Dogs are allergic to many foods that are best-sellers and highly recommended by breeders and veterinary surgeons. Changing the brand of food that you buy may not eliminate the problem if the element to which the dog is allergic is contained in the new brand.

Recognising a food allergy is difficult. Humans vomit or have rashes when they eat a food to which they are allergic. Dogs neither vomit nor (usually) develop a rash. They react in the same manner as they do to an airborne or flea allergy: they itch, scratch and bite, thus making the diagnosis extremely difficult. Whilst pollen allergies and parasite bites are usually season-al, food allergies are year-round problems.

FOOD INTOLERANCE
Food intolerance is the inability of the dog to completely digest certain foods. Puppies that may have done very well on their mother's milk may not do well on cow's milk. The result of this food intolerance may be loose bowels, passing gas and stomach pains. These are the only obvious symptoms of food intolerance and that makes diagnosis difficult.

Border Collies pick up fleas and ticks because they spend so much time in grass where these parasites hide awaiting a suitable host.

TREATING FOOD PROBLEMS

It is possible to handle food allergies and food intolerance yourself. Put your dog on a diet that it has never had. Obviously if it has never eaten this new food it can't have been allergic or intolerant of it. Start with a single ingredient that is not in the dog's diet at the present time. Ingredients like chopped beef or fish are common in dog's diets, so try something more exotic like ostrich, rabbit, pheasant or even just vegetables. Keep the dog on this diet (with no additives) for a month. If the symptoms of food allergy or intolerance disappear, chances are your dog has a food allergy.

Don't think that the single ingredient cured the problem. You still must find a suitable diet and ascertain which ingredient in the old diet was objectionable. This is most easily done by adding ingredients to the new diet one at a time. Let the dog stay on the modified diet for a month before you add another ingredient. Eventually, you will determine the ingredient that caused the adverse reaction.

An alternative method is to carefully study the ingredients in the diet to which your dog is allergic or intolerable. Identify the main ingredient in this diet and eliminate the main ingredient by buying a different food that does not have that ingredient. Keep experimenting until the symptoms disappear after one month on the new diet.

Know what your dog is eating ! Read the ingredients of everything you feed your Border Collie.

**The two photos above show normal dog hairs magnified 60-150 times their actual size.
The two lower photos show distressed hairs that are smashed (right) or frayed (left).**

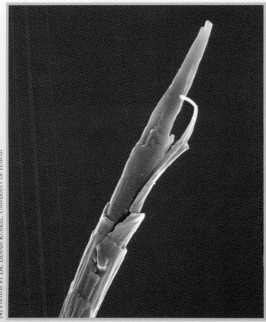

A scanning electron micrograph (S. E. M.) of a dog flea, *Ctenocephalides canis*.

S. E. M. BY DR DENNIS KUNKEL, UNIVERSITY OF HAWAII

(Facing Page) A scanning electron micrograph of a dog or cat flea, *Ctenocephalides*, magnified more than 100x. This has been colourised for effect.

Magnified head of a dog flea, *Ctenocephalides canis*.

EXTERNAL PARASITES

Of all the problems to which dogs are prone, none is more well known and frustrating than fleas. Fleas, as well as ticks and mites, are difficult to prevent but relatively simple to cure. Parasites that are

DID YOU KNOW?

Fleas have been around for millions of years and have adapted to changing host animals.

They are able to go through a complete life cycle in less than one month or they can extend their lives to almost two years by remaining as pupae or cocoons. They do not need blood or any other food for up to 20 months.

They have been measured as being able to jump 300,000 times and can jump 150 times their length in any direction including straight up. Those are just a few of the reasons they are so successful in infesting a dog!

harboured inside the body are more difficult to cure but they are easier to control.

FLEAS

To control a flea infestation you have to understand the life cycle of a typical flea. Fleas are basically a summertime problem and their effective treatment (destruction) is environmental. There is no single flea-control medicine (insecticide) that can be used in every flea-infested area. To understand flea control you must apply suitable treatment to the weak link in the life cycle of the flea.

THE LIFE CYCLE OF A FLEA

Fleas are found in four forms: eggs, larvae, pupae and adults. You really need a low-power microscope or hand lens to identify a living flea's eggs, pupae or larva. They spend

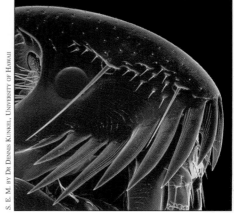

S. E. M. BY DR DENNIS KUNKEL, UNIVERSITY OF HAWAII

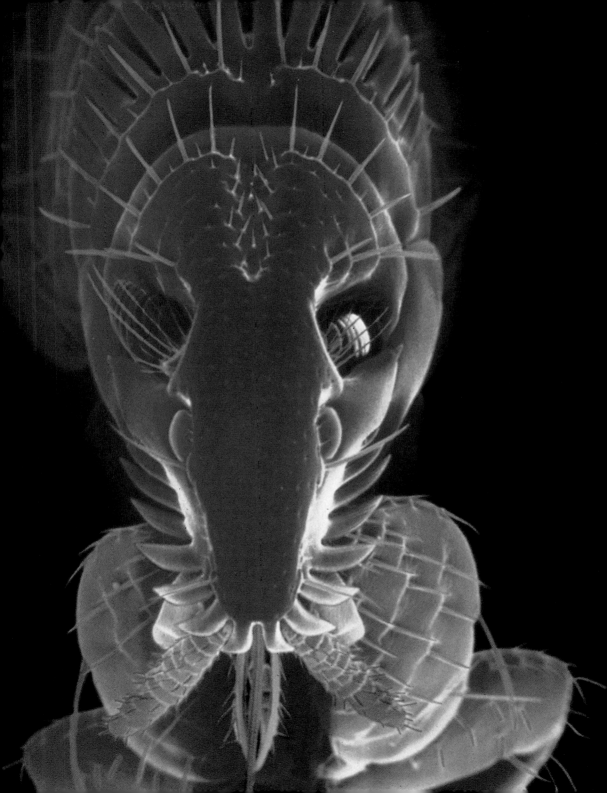

The Life Cycle of the Flea

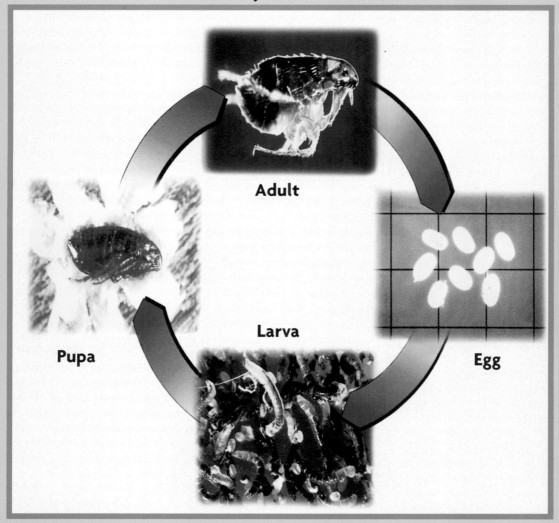

Adult

Pupa

Larva

Egg

The life cycle of the flea was posterised by Fleabusters®. Poster Courtesy of Fleabusters®, R$_x$ for Fleas.

their whole lives on your dog unless they are forcibly removed by brushing, bathing, scratching or biting.

The dog flea is scientifically known as *Ctenocephalides canis* whilst the cat flea is called *Ctenocephalides felis*. Several species infest both dogs and cats.

Fleas lay eggs whilst they are in residence upon your dog. These eggs fall off almost as

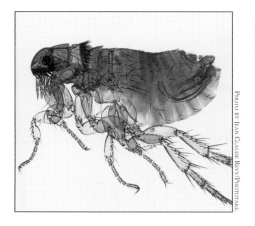

Photo by Jean Claude Revy/Phototake.

DID YOU KNOW?

There are many parasiticides which can be used around your home and garden to control fleas.

Natural pyrethrins can be used inside the house.

Allethrin, bioallethrin, permethrin and resmethrin can also be used inside the house but permethrin has been used successfully outdoors, too.

Carbaryl can be used indoors and outdoors.

Propoxur can be used indoors.

Chlorpyrifos, diazinon and malathion can be used indoors or outdoors and it has an extended residual activity.

soon as they dry (they may be a bit damp when initially laid) and are the reservoir of future flea infestations. If your dog scratches himself and is able to dislodge a few fleas, they simply fall off and await a future chance to attack a dog...or even a person. Yes, fleas from dogs bite people. That's why it is so important to control fleas both on the dog and in the dog's entire environment. You must, therefore, treat the dog and the environment simultaneously.

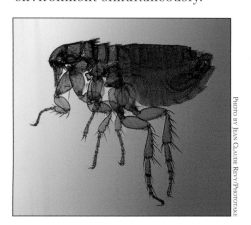

Photo by Jean Claude Revy/Phototake.

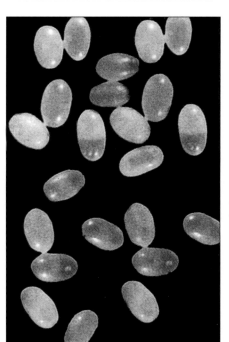

The eggs of the dog flea.

Male cat fleas, *Ctenocephalides felis*, are very commonly found on dogs.

111

Dwight R. Kuhn's magnificent action photo showing a flea jumping from a dog's back.

Photo by Dwight R. Kuhn

DE-FLEAING THE HOME
Cleanliness is the simple rule. If you have a cat living with your dog, the matter is more complicated since most dog fleas are actually cat fleas. Cats climb onto many areas that are never accessible to dogs (like window sills, table tops, etc.), so

Human lice look like dog lice; the two are closely related.

Photo by Dwight R. Kuhn

you have to clean all of these areas. The hard floor surfaces (tiles, wood, stone and linoleum) must be mopped several times a day. Drops of food onto the floor are actually food for flea larvae! All rugs and furniture must be vacuumed several times a day. Don't forget closets, under furniture and cushions. A study has reported that a vacuum cleaner with a beater bar can remove only 20 percent of the larvae and 50 percent of the eggs. The vacuum bags should be discarded

DID YOU KNOW?

Ivermectin is quickly becoming the drug of choice for treating many parasitic skin diseases in dogs.

For some unknown reason, herding dogs like Border Collies, Old English Sheepdogs and German Shepherds, etc., are extremely sensitive to ivermectin.

Ivermectin injections have killed some dogs, but dogs heavily infected with skin disorders may be treated anyway.

The ivermectin reaction is a toxicosis that causes tremors, loss of power to move their muscles, prolonged dilatation of the pupil of the eye, coma (unconsciousness), or cessation of breathing (death).

The toxicosis usually starts from 4-6 hours after ingestion (not injection), but can begin as late as 12 hours. The longer it takes to set in, the milder is the reaction.

Ivermectin should only be prescribed and administered by a vet. Some ivermectin treatments require two doses.

mops, you have to treat the outdoor range of your dog. When trimming bushes and spreading insecticide, be careful not to poison areas in which fishes or other animals reside. Remember to choose dog-safe insecticides, but to be absolutely sure, keep your dog away from treated areas.

into a sealed plastic bag or burned. The vacuum machine itself should be cleaned. The outdoor area to which your dog has access must also be treated with an insecticide.

Your vet will be able to recommend a household insecticidal spray, but this must be used with caution and instructions strictly adhered to.

There are many drugs available to kill fleas on the dog itself, such as ivermectin, and it is best to have the de-fleaing and de-worming supervised by your vet. Ivermectin may not be recommended for the Border Collie since herding dogs are sensitive to the drug; it can possibly kill them. Ivermectin is effective against many external and internal parasites including heartworms, roundworms, tapeworms, flukes, ticks and mites. It has not been approved for use to control these pests, but veterinary surgeons frequently use it anyway. Ivermectin may not be available in all areas.

STERILISING THE ENVIRONMENT
Besides cleaning your home with vacuum cleaners and

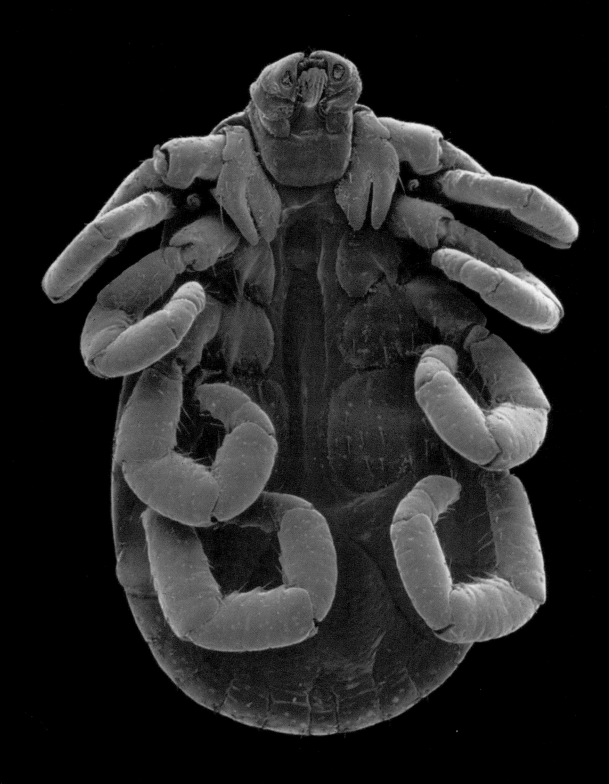

TICKS AND MITES

Though not as common as fleas, ticks and mites are found all over the tropical and temperate world. They don't bite like fleas, they harpoon. They dig their sharp proboscis (nose) into the dog's skin and drink the blood, which is their only food and drink. Dogs can get paralysis, Lyme disease, Rocky Mountain spotted fever (normally found in the U.S.A. only), and many other diseases from ticks and mites. They may live where fleas are found but they also like to hide in cracks or seams in walls wherever dogs live. They are controlled the same way fleas are controlled.

The tick *Dermacentor variabilis* may well be the most common dog tick in many geographical areas, especially where the climate is hot and humid.

Most dog ticks have life expectancies of a week to six months, depending upon climatic conditions. They neither jump nor fly, but crawl slowly and can range up to 5 metres 16 feet) to reach a sleeping or unsuspecting dog.

MANGE

Mange is a skin irritation caused by mites. Some mites are contagious, like *Cheyletiella*, ear mites, scabies and chiggers. The non-contagious mites are *Demodex*. The most serious of the mites is the one that causes ear-mite infestation. Ear mites are usually controlled with ivermectin.

It is essential that your dog be treated for mange as quickly as possible because some forms of mange are transmissible to people.

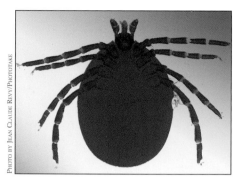

An uncommon dog tick of the genus *Ixode*. Magnified 10x.

PHOTO BY JEAN CLAUDE REVY/PHOTOTAKE.

(Facing Page) The dog tick, *Dermacentor variabilis*, is probably the most common tick found on dogs. Look at the strength in its eight legs! No wonder it's hard to detach them.

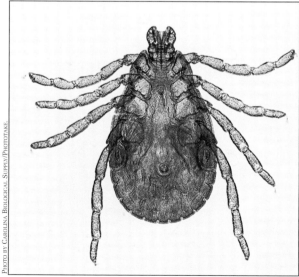

PHOTO BY CAROLINA BIOLOGICAL SUPPLY/PHOTOTAKE.

A brown dog tick, *Rhipicephalus sanguineus*, is an uncommon but annoying tick found on dogs.

S. E. M. BY DR DENNIS KUNKEL, UNIVERSITY OF HAWAII.

A deer tick, the carrier of Lyme disease.

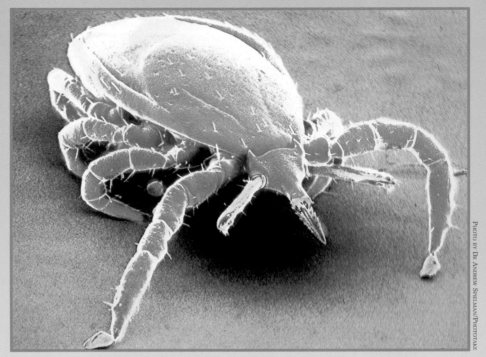

Magnified view of the mange mite, *Psoroptes bovis.*

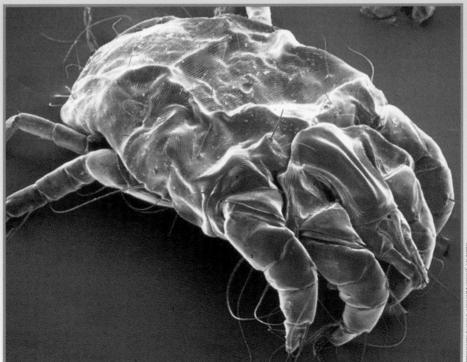

INTERNAL PARASITES

Most animals—fishes, birds and mammals, including dogs and humans—have worms and other parasites that live inside their bodies. According to Dr Herbert R. Axelrod, the fish pathologist, there are two kinds of parasites: dumb and smart. The smart parasites live in peaceful cooperation with their hosts (symbiosis), whilst the dumb parasites kill their host. Most of the worm infections are relatively easy to control. If they are not controlled they eventually weaken the host dog to the point that other medical problems occur, but they are not dumb parasites that directly cause the death of their hosts.

ROUNDWORMS

The roundworms that infect dogs are scientifically known as *Toxocara canis*. They live in the dog's intestine and shed eggs continually. It has been estimated that an average-sized dog produces about 150 grammes of faeces every day. Each gramme of faeces averages 10,000–12,000 eggs of roundworms. All areas in which dogs

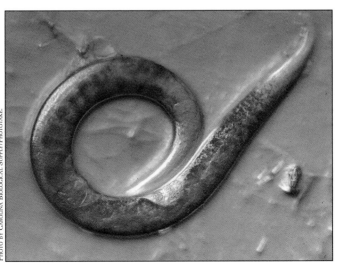

PHOTO BY CAROLINA BIOLOGICAL SUPPLY/PHOTOTAKE.

The roundworm can infect both dogs and humans.

117

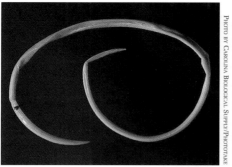

The roundworm *Rhabditis*.

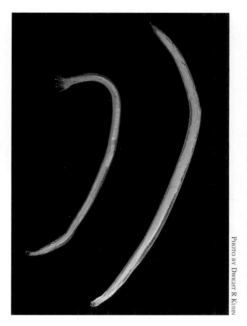

Male and female hookworms, *Ancylostoma caninum*, are uncommonly found in pet or show dogs in Britain. Hookworms may infect other dogs that have exposure to grasslands.

roam contain astronomical numbers of roundworm eggs. The greatest danger of roundworms is that they infect people, too! It is wise to have your dog tested regularly for roundworms.

Pigs also have roundworm infections that can be passed to humans and dogs. The typical pig roundworm parasite is called *Ascaris lumbricoides*.

HOOKWORMS

The worm *Ancylostoma caninum* is commonly called the dog hookworm. It is also dangerous to humans and cats. It attaches itself

to the dog's intestines by its teeth. It changes the site of its attachment about six times a day, and the dog loses blood from each detachment. This blood loss can cause iron-deficiency anaemia. Hookworms are easily purged from the dog with many medications, the best of which seems to be ivermectin even though it has not been approved for such use, nor is it recommended for herding dogs.

In Britain the 'temperate climate' hookworm (*Uncinaria stenocephala*) is rarely found in pet or show dogs, but can occur in hunting packs, racing Greyhounds and sheepdogs because these hookworms can be prevalent wherever dogs are exercised regularly on grassland.

> **DID YOU KNOW?**
> Caring for the puppy starts before the puppy is born by keeping the dam healthy and well-nourished. Most puppies have worms, even if they are not evident, so a worming programme is essential. The worms continually shed eggs except during their dormant stage, when they just rest in the tissues of the puppy. During this stage they are not evident during a routine examination.

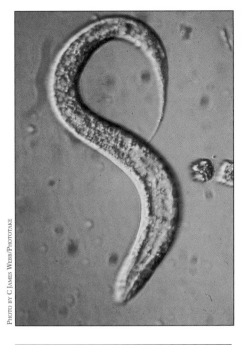

The infective stage of the hookworm larva.

PHOTO BY C JAMES WEBB/PHOTOTAKE

DID YOU KNOW?

Average size dogs can pass 1,360,000 roundworm eggs every day.

For example, if there were only 1 million dogs in the world, the world would be saturated with 1,300 metric tonnes of dog faeces. These faeces would contain 15,000,000,000 roundworm eggs.

7 to 31 percent of home gardens and children's play boxes in the U. S. contained roundworm eggs.

Flushing dog's faeces down the toilet is not a safe practice because the usual sewage treatments do not destroy roundworm eggs.

Infected puppies start shedding roundworm eggs at 3 weeks of age. They can be infected by their mother's milk.

TAPEWORMS

There are many species of tapeworms, many of which are carried by fleas! The dog eats the flea and starts the tapeworm cycle. Humans can also be infected with tapeworms, so don't eat fleas! Fleas are so small that your dog could pass them onto your hands, your plate or your food and make it possible for you to ingest a flea which is carrying tapeworm eggs.

Whilst tapeworm infection is not life threatening in dogs (smart parasite!), it can be the cause of a very serious liver disease for humans. About 50 percent of the humans infected with *Echinococcus multilocularis*, causing alveolar hydatis, perish.

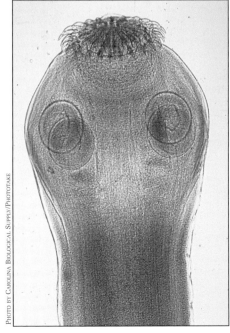

The head and rostellum (the round prominence on the scolex) of a tapeworm, which infects dogs and humans.

PHOTO BY CAROLINA BIOLOGICAL SUPPLY/PHOTOTAKE

119

Humans, rats, squirrels, foxes, coyotes, wolves, mixed breeds of dogs and purebred dogs are all susceptible to tapeworm infection. Except in humans, tapeworms are usually not a fatal infection. Infected individuals can harbour a thousand parasitic worms. Tapeworms have two sexes—male and female (many other worms have only one sex—male and female in the same worm). If dogs eat infected rats or mice, they get the tapeworm disease.

One month after attaching to a dog's intestine, the worm starts shedding eggs. These eggs are infective immediately. Infective eggs can live for a few months without a host animal. Roundworms, whipworms and tapeworms are just a few of the other commonly known worms that infect dogs.

HEARTWORMS

Heartworms are thin, extended worms up to 30 cms (12 ins) long that live in a dog's heart and the major blood vessels around it. Your pet may have up to 200 of these worms. The symptoms may be loss of energy, loss of appetite, coughing, the development of a pot belly and anaemia.

Heartworms are transmitted by mosquitoes. The mosquito drinks the blood of an infected dog and takes in larvae with the blood. The larvae, called microfilaria, develop within the body of the mosquito and are passed on to the next dog bitten after the larvae mature. It takes two to three weeks for the larvae to develop to the infective stage within the body of the mosquito. Dogs should be treated at about six weeks of age, then every six months.

Blood testing for heartworms is not necessarily indicative of how seriously your dog is infected. This is a dangerous disease. Dogs in the United Kingdom are not affected by heartworm.

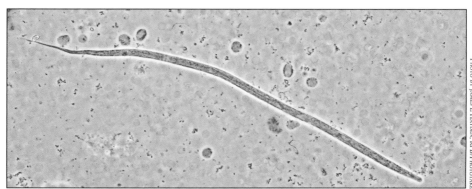

The heartworm, *Dirofilaria immitis.*

PHOTO BY JAMES E HAYDEN, RPB/PHOTOTAKE

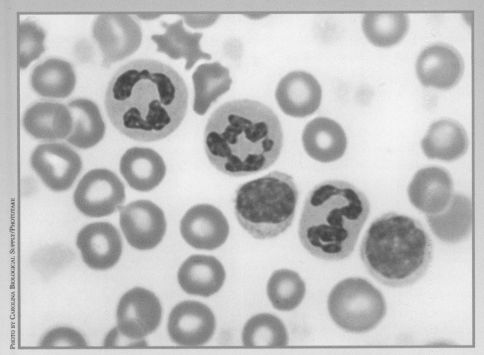

Magnified heartworm larvae, *Dirofilaria immitis.*

The heart of a dog infected with canine heartworm, *Dirofilaria immitis.*

First Aid
at a Glance

Burns
Place the affected area under cool water;
use ice if only a small area is burnt.

Bee/Insect bites
Apply ice to relieve swelling; antihista-
mine dosed properly.

Animal bites
Clean any bleeding area; apply pressure
until bleeding subsides; go to the vet.

Spider bites
Use cold compress and a pressurised
pack to inhibit venom's spreading.

Antifreeze poisoning
Immediately induce vomiting by using
hydrogen peroxide.

Fish hooks
Removal best handled by vet;
hook must be cut in order to remove.

Snake bites
Pack ice around bite; contact vet
quickly; identify snake for proper
antivenin.

Car accident
Move dog from roadway with blanket;
seek veterinary aid.

Shock
Calm the dog, keep him warm; seek
immediate veterinary help.

Nosebleed
Apply cold compress to the nose; apply
pressure to any visible abrasion.

Bleeding
Apply pressure above the area; treat
wound by applying a cotton pack.

Heat stroke
Submerge dog in cold bath; cool down
with fresh air and water; go to the vet.

Frostbite/Hypothermia
Warm the dog with a warm bath, electric
blankets or hot water bottles.

Abrasions
Clean the wound and wash out
thoroughly with fresh water;
apply antiseptic.

 *Remember: an injured dog may attempt
to bite a helping hand from fear and confusion.
Always muzzle the dog before trying to offer assistance.*

Border Collie

The term old is a qualitative term. For dogs, as well as their masters, old is relative. Certainly we can all distinguish between a puppy Border Collie and an adult Border Collie—there are the obvious physical traits, such as size, appearance and facial expressions, and personality traits. Puppies that are nasty are very rare. Puppies and young dogs like to play with children. Children's natural exuberance is a good match for the seemingly endless energy of young dogs. They like to run, jump, chase and retrieve. When dogs grow up and cease their interaction with

DID YOU KNOW?

The bottom line is simply that a dog is getting old when YOU think it is getting old because it slows down in its general activities, including walking, running, eating, jumping and retrieving. On the other hand, certain activities increase, like more sleeping, more barking and more repetition of habits like going to the door when you put your coat on without being called.

children, they are often thought of as being too old to play with the kids.

On the other hand, if a Border Collie is only exposed to people over 60 years of age, its life will

The Border Collie enjoys a life span of about 14 years, which is an impressive life expectancy for any dog.

normally be less active and it will not seem to be getting old as its activity level slows down.

If people live to be 100 years old, dogs live to be 20 years old. Whilst this is a good rule of thumb, it is very inaccurate. When trying to compare dog years to human years, you cannot make a generalisation about all dogs. You can make the generalisation that, 14 years is a good life span for a Border Collie, which is quite good compared to many other purebred dogs that may only live to 8 or 9 years of age. Some

When your dog refuses to climb the stairs that he has climbed for years, you will know that he is 'not the dog he used to be.' Treat seniors with extra care.

DID YOU KNOW?

An old dog starts to show one or more of the following symptoms:

• The hair on its face and paws starts to turn grey. The colour breakdown usually starts around the eyes and mouth.

• Sleep patterns are deeper and longer and the old dog is harder to awaken.

• Food intake diminishes.

• Responses to calls, whistles and other signals are ignored more and more.

• Eye contacts do not evoke tail wagging (assuming they once did).

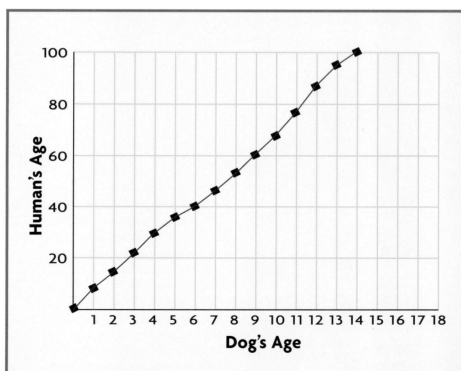

Border Collies have been known to live to 20 years. Dogs are generally considered mature within three years, but they can reproduce even earlier. So the first three years of a dog's life are like seven times that of comparable humans. That means a 3-year-old dog is like a 21-year-old human. As the curve of comparison shows, there is no hard and fast rule for comparing dog and human ages. The comparison is made even more difficult, for not all humans age at the same rate...and human females live longer than human males.

WHAT TO LOOK FOR IN SENIORS

Most veterinary surgeons and behaviourists use the seventh year mark as the time to consider a dog a 'senior.' The term 'senior' does not imply that the dog is geriatric and has begun to fail in mind and body. Ageing is essentially a slowing process. Humans readily admit that they feel a difference in their activity level from age 20 to

> **DID YOU KNOW?**
>
> The symptoms listed below are symptoms that gradually appear and become more noticeable. They are not life threatening, however, the symptoms below are to be taken very seriously and a discussion with your veterinary surgeon is warranted:
>
> • Your dog cries and whimpers when it moves and stops running completely.
>
> • Convulsions start or become more serious and frequent. The usual convulsion (spasm) is when the dog stiffens and starts to tremble being unable or unwilling to move. The seizure usually lasts for 5 to 30 minutes.
>
> • Your dog drinks more water and urinates more frequently. Wetting and bowel accidents take place indoors without warning.
>
> • Vomiting becomes more and more frequent.

30, and then from 30 to 40, etc. By treating the seven-year-old dog as a senior, owners are able to implement certain therapeutic and preventive medical strategies with the help of their veterinary surgeons. A senior-care programme should include at least two veterinary visits per year, screening sessions to determine the dog's health status, as well as nutritional counselling. Veterinary surgeons determine the senior dog's health status through

It is usually difficult for a dog's owner to realise that his dog is getting old since the changes are so gradual. Seniors should be examined by a vet twice yearly to ensure the best care possible.

125

a blood smear for a complete blood count, serum chemistry profile with electrolytes, urinalysis, blood pressure check, electrocardiogram, ocular tonometry (pressure on the eyeball), and dental prophylaxis.

Your senior Border Collie needs your patience and good care more than ever.

Such an extensive programme for senior dogs is well advised before owners start to see the obvious physical signs of ageing, such as slower and inhibited movement, greying, increased sleep/nap periods, and disinterest in play and other activity. This preventative programme promises a longer, healthier life for the ageing dog. Amongst the physical problems common in ageing dogs are the loss of sight and hearing, arthritis, kidney and liver failure, diabetes mellitus, heart disease, and Cushing's disease (a hormonal disease).

In addition to the physical manifestations discussed, there are some behavioural changes and problems related to ageing dogs. Dogs suffering from hearing or vision loss, dental discomfort or arthritis can become aggressive. Likewise the near-deaf and/or blind dog may be startled more easily and react in an unexpectedly aggressive manner. Seniors suffering from senility can become more impatient and irritable. Housesoiling accidents are associated with loss of mobility, kidney problems, loss of sphincter control as well as plaque accumulation, physiological brain changes, and reactions to medications. Older dogs, just like young puppies, suffer from separation anxiety, which can lead to excessive barking, whining, housesoiling, and destructive behaviour. Seniors may become fearful of everyday sounds, such as vacuum cleaners, heaters, thunder, and passing traffic. Some dogs have difficulty sleeping, due to discomfort, the need for frequent potty visits, and the like. Owners should avoid spoiling the older dog with too many fatty treats. Obesity is a common problem in older dogs and subtracts years from their lifespan. Keep the senior dog as trim as possible since excessive weight puts additional stress on the body's vital organs. Some breeders recommend supplementing the diet with foods high in fibre and lower in calories. Adding fresh vegetables and marrow broth to the senior's diet makes a tasty, low-calorie, low-fat supplement. Vets also offer specialty diets for senior dogs that are worth exploring.

Your dog, as he nears his twilight years, needs his owner's

patience and good care more than ever. Never punish an older dog for an accident or abnormal behaviour. For all the years of love, protection and companionship that your dog has provided, he deserves special attention and courtesies. The older dog may need to relieve himself at 3 a.m. because he can no longer hold it for eight hours. Older dogs may not be able to remain crated for more than two or three hours. It may be time to give up a sofa or chair to your old friend. Although he may not seem as enthusiastic about your attention and petting, he does appreciate the considerations you offer as he gets older.

Your Border Collie does not understand why his world is slowing down. Owners must make the transition into the golden years as pleasant and rewarding as possible.

WHAT TO DO WHEN THE TIME COMES

You are never fully prepared to make a rational decision about putting your dog to sleep. It is very obvious that you love your Border Collie or you would not be reading this book. Putting a loved dog to sleep is extremely difficult. It is a decision that must be made with your veterinary surgeon. You are usually forced to make the decision when one of the life-threatening symptoms listed above becomes serious enough for you to seek medical (veterinary) help.

If the prognosis of the malady indicates the end is near and your

If you are interested in burying your dog, there are pet cemeteries catering to pet lovers.

127

beloved pet will only suffer more and experience no enjoyment for the balance of its life, then euthanasia is the right choice.

What is Euthanasia?

Euthanasia derives from the Greek meaning good death. In other words, it means the planned, painless killing of a dog suffering from a painful, incurable condition, or who is so aged that it cannot walk, see, eat or control its excretory functions.

Euthanasia is usually accomplished by injection with an overdose of an anaesthesia or barbiturate. Aside from the prick of the needle, the experience is painless.

How About You?

The decision to euthanize your dog is never easy. The days during which the dog becomes ill and the end occurs can be unusually stressful for you. If this is your first experience with the death of a loved one, you may need the comfort dictated by your religious beliefs. If you are the head of the family and have children, you should have involved them in the decision of putting your Border Collie to sleep. Usually your dog can be maintained on drugs for a few days whilst it is kept in the clinic in order to give you ample time to make a decision. During this time, talking with members of the family or religious representatives, or even people who have lived through this same experience, can ease the burden of your inevitable decision. In any case, euthanasia is painful and stressful for the family of the dog. Unfortunately, it does not end there.

The Final Resting Place

Dogs can have the same privileges as humans. They can be buried in a pet cemetery in a burial container (very expensive); buried in your garden in a place suitably marked with a stone, newly planted tree or bush; cremated with the ashes being given to you, or even stuffed and mounted by a taxidermist.

All of these options should be discussed frankly and openly with your veterinary surgeon. Do not be afraid to ask financial questions. Cremations are usually mass burnings and the ashes you get may not be only the ashes of your beloved dog. If you want a private cremation, there are small crematoriums available to all veterinary clinics. Your vet can usually arrange for this but it may be a little more expensive.

GETTING ANOTHER DOG?

The grief of losing your beloved dog will be as lasting as the grief of losing a human friend or relative. You cannot go out and buy another grandfather, but you can go out and buy another Border Collie. In most cases, if your dog died of old age (if there is such a thing), it had slowed down considerably. Do you want

a new Border Collie puppy to replace it? Or are you better off in finding a more mature Border Collie, say two to three years of age, which will usually be housetrained and will have an already developed personality. In this case, you can find out if you

A resting place for your dog's ashes may be available locally. Contact your veterinary surgeon or local dog club for more information.

like each other after a few hours of being together.

The decision is, of course, your own. Do you want another Border Collie? Perhaps you want a smaller or larger dog? How much do you want to spend on a dog? Look in your local newspapers for advertisements (DOGS FOR SALE), or, better yet, consult your local society for the prevention of cruelty to animals to adopt a dog. It is harder to find puppies at an animal shelter, but there are often many adult dogs in need of new homes. You may be able to find another Border Collie, or you may choose another breed or a mixed-breed dog. Private breeders are the best source for high-quality puppies and dogs.

The decision to replace a lost pet is a very personal one. When youngsters are involved, the new Border Collie pup will help fill the gap left by the deceased pet.

Whatever you decide, do it as quickly as possible. Most people usually buy the same breed because they know (and love) the characteristics of that breed. Then, too, they often know people who have the same breed and perhaps they are lucky enough that one of their friends expects a litter soon. What could be better?

> **DID YOU KNOW?**
> The more open discussion you have about the whole stressful occurrence, the easier it will be for you when the time comes.

129

CDS: COGNITIVE DYSFUNCTION SYNDROME
"Old Dog Syndrome"

There are many ways to evaluate old-dog syndrome. Veterinary surgeons have defined CDS (cognitive dysfunction syndrome) as the gradual deterioration of cognitive abilities. These are indicated by changes in the dog's behaviour. When a dog changes its routine response, and maladies have been eliminated as the cause of these behavioural changes, then CDS is the usual diagnosis.

More than half the dogs over 8 years old suffer some form of CDS. The older the dog, the more chance it has of suffering from CDS. In humans, doctors often dismiss the CDS behavioural changes as part of 'winding down.'

There are four major signs of CDS: frequent toilet accidents inside the home, sleeps much more or much less than normal, acts confused, and fails to respond to social stimuli.

SYMPTOMS OF CDS

FREQUENT TOILET ACCIDENTS
- *Urinates in the house.*
- *Defecates in the house.*
- *Doesn't signal that he wants to go out.*

SLEEP PATTERNS
- *Moves much more slowly.*
- *Sleeps more than normal during the day.*
- *Sleeps less during the night.*
- *Walks around listlessly and without a destination goal.*

CONFUSION
- *Goes outside and just stands there.*
- *Appears confused with a faraway look in his eyes.*
- *Hides more often.*
- *Doesn't recognise friends.*
- *Doesn't come when called.*

FAILS TO RESPOND TO SOCIAL STIMULI
- *Comes to people less frequently, whether called or not.*
- *Doesn't tolerate petting for more than a short time.*
- *Doesn't come to the door when you return home from work.*

SHOWING YOUR
Border Collie

When you purchased your Border Collie you will have made it clear to the breeder whether you wanted one just as a loveable companion and pet, or if you hoped to be buying a Border Collie with show prospects. No reputable breeder will have sold you a young puppy saying that it was definitely of show quality for so much can go wrong during the early weeks and months of a puppy's development. If you plan to show what you will hopefully have acquired is a puppy with 'show potential'.

The first concept that the canine novice learns when watching a dog show is that each breed first competes against members of its own breed. Once the judge has selected the best member of each breed, then that chosen dog will compete with other dogs in its group. Finally

the best of each group will compete for Best in Show and Reserve Best in Show.

The second concept that you must understand is that the dogs

Whilst the Border Collie's favourite forum may be the sheepdog trial, many handsome dogs excel in the show ring. This is a happy day for this winning duo.

are not actually competing with one another. The judge compares each dog against the breed standard, which is a written description of the ideal specimen of the breed. This imaginary dog never walked into a show ring, has never been bred and, to the woe of dog breeders around the globe, does not exist. Breeders attempt to get as close to this

DID YOU KNOW?

The Kennel Club divides its dogs into seven Groups: Gundogs, Utility, Working, Toy, Terrier, Hounds and Pastoral.*

*The Pastoral Group, established in 1999, includes those sheepdog breeds previously categorised in the Working Group.

ideal as possible, with every litter, but theoretically the 'perfect' dog is so elusive that it is impossible. (And if the 'perfect' dog were born, breeders and judges would never agree that it was indeed 'perfect.')

If you are interested in exploring dog shows, your best bet is to join your local breed club. These clubs host shows (often matches and open shows for beginners), send out newsletters, offer training days and provide an outlet to meet members who are often friendly and generous with their advice and contacts. To locate the nearest breed club for you, contact The Kennel Club, the ruling body for the British dog world. The Kennel Club governs not only conformation shows but also working trials, obedience trials, agility trials and field trials. The Kennel Club furnishes the rules and regulations for all these events plus general dog registration and other basic requirements of dog ownership. Its annual show called the Crufts Dogs Show, held in Birmingham, is the largest bench show in England. Every year no fewer than 20,000 of the U.K.'s best dogs qualify to participate in this marvellous show which lasts four days.

The Kennel Club governs many different kinds of shows in Great Britain, Australia, South Africa and beyond. At the most competitive and prestigious of these shows, the Championship Shows, a dog can earn Challenge Certificates, and thereby become a Show Champion or a Champion. A dog must earn three Challenge Certificates under three different judges to earn the prefix of 'Sh Ch.' or 'Ch.' Some breeds must qualify in a field trial in order to gain the title of full champion. Challenge Certificates are awarded to a very small percentage of the dogs competing. The number of Challenge Certificates awarded in any one year is based upon the total number of dogs in each breed entered for competition.

There are three types of Championship shows: an all-breed General Championship show for all Kennel-Club-recognised breeds; a Group

WINNING THE TICKET

Earning a championship at Kennel Club shows is the most difficult in the world. Compared to the United States and Canada where it is relatively not 'challenging,' collecting three green tickets not only requires much time and effort, it can be very expensive! Challenge Certificates, as the tickets are properly known, are the building blocks of champions—good breeding, good handling, good training and good luck!

Championship show, limited to breeds within one of the Groups; and a Breed Show, usually confined to a single breed. The Kennel Club determines which breeds at which Championship Shows will have the opportunity to earn Challenge Certificates (or tickets). Serious exhibitors often will opt not to participate if the tickets are withheld at a particular show. This policy makes earning championships ever more difficult to accomplish.

Open Shows are generally less competitive and are frequently used as 'practice shows' for young dogs. There are hundreds of Open Shows each year that can be

During the show, treats are often used to capture the dog's attention.

invitingly social events and are great first show experiences for the novice. Even if you're considering just watching a show to wet your paws, an Open Show is a great choice.

Whilst Championship and Open Shows are most important for the beginner to understand, there are other types of shows in which the interested dog owner can participate. Training clubs sponsor Matches that can be entered on the day of the show for a nominal fee. In these introductory-level exhibitions, two dogs are pulled from a raffle and 'matched,' the winner of that match goes on to the next round, and eventually only one dog is left undefeated.

Exemption Shows are similar in that they are simply fun classes and usually held in conjunction with small agricultural shows.

> ### DID YOU KNOW?
> Just like with anything else, there is a certain etiquette to the show ring that can only be learned through experience. Showing your dog can be quite intimidating to you as a novice when it seems as if everyone else knows what he's doing. You can familiarise yourself with ring procedure beforehand by taking a class to prepare you and your dog for conformation showing or by talking with an experienced handler. When you are in the ring, listen and pay attention to the judge and follow his/her directions. Remember, even the most skilled handlers had to start somewhere. Keep it up and you too will become a proficient handler before too long!

Primary shows can also be entered on the day of the event and dogs entered must not have won anything towards their titles. Sanction shows and Limited shows must be entered well in advance, and there are limitations upon who can enter. Regardless of which type you choose, you and your dog will have a grand time competing and learning your way about the shows.

Before you actually step into the ring, you would be well advised to sit back and observe the judge's ring procedure. If it is your first time in the ring, do not be over-anxious and run to the front of the line. It is much better to stand back and study how the exhibitor in front of you is performing. The judge asks each handler to 'stand' the dog, hopefully showing the dog off to his best advantage. The judge will observe the dog from a distance and from different angles, approach the dog, check his teeth, overall structure, alertness and muscle tone, as well as consider how well the dog 'conforms' to the standard. Most importantly,

Few breeds excel at agility trials like the Border Collie. Agility trials are amongst the most popular events for Border Collies and their owners.

Running a weave course, weaving in and out of upright stakes, is one of the events at agility trials. Winning requires the fastest and most flawless performance.

the judge will have the exhibitor move the dog around the ring in some pattern that he or she should specify (another advantage to not going first, but always listen since some judges change their directions, and the judge is always right!). Finally the judge will give the dog one last look before moving on to the next exhibitor.

If you are not in the top three at your first show, do not be discouraged. Be patient and consistent and you will eventually find yourself in the winning lineup. Remember that the winners were once in your shoes and have devoted many hours and much money to earn the placement. If you find that your dog is losing every time and never getting a nod, it may be time to consider a different dog sport or just enjoy your Border Collie as a pet.

WORKING TRIALS
Working trials can be entered by any well-trained dog of any breed, not just Gundogs or Working dogs. Many dogs that earn the Kennel Club Good Citizen Dog award choose to participate in a working trial. There are five stakes at both open and championship levels:

135

Tending sheep is what Border Collies are all about. Sheepdog trials take advantage of the dogs' natural desire to work livestock.

Companion Dog (CD), Utility Dog (UD), Working Dog (WD), Tracking Dog (TD), and Patrol Dog (PD). Like in conformation shows, dogs compete against a standard and if the dog reaches the qualifying mark, it obtains a certificate.

Going through a collapsed tunnel is a difficult obstacle for many dogs, but this Border Collie handled the task gleefully.

Divided into groups, each exercise must be achieved 70 percent in order to qualify. If the dog achieves 80 percent in the open level, it receives a Certificate of Merit (COM), in the championship level, it receives a Qualifying Certificate. At the CD stake, dogs must participate in four groups, Control, Stay, Agility and Search (Retrieve and Nosework). At the next three levels, UD, WD and TD, there are only three groups: Control, Agility and Nosework.

Agility consists of three jumps: a vertical scale up a six-foot wall of planks; a clear jump over a basic three-foot hurdle with a removable top bar; and a long jump across angled planks stretching nine feet.

To earn the UD, WD and TD, dogs must track approximately one-half mile for articles laid from one-half hour to three hours ago. Tracks consist of turns and legs, and fresh ground is used for each participant.

The fifth stake, PD, involves teaching manwork, which is not recommended for every breed.

HOW TO ENTER A DOG SHOW
1. Obtain an entry form and show schedule from the Show Secretary.
2. Select the classes that you want to enter and complete the entry form.
3. Transfer your dog into your name at The Kennel Club. (Be sure that this matter is handled before entering.)
4. Find out how far in advance show entries must be made. Oftentimes it's more than a couple of months.

SHEEPDOG TRIALS

Since the first sheepdog trial recorded in the late nineteenth century in Wales, the practice of sheepdog trials has grown tremendously. Border Collies, without a doubt, dominate this arena of the dog sport. This first trial began as a friendly match to see which farmer's dog was the best at moving sheep. Today the sport is more organised than those early days. The International Sheep Dog Society holds four National Trials each year held in Great Britain. These trials are held in England, Ireland, Scotland and Wales. The International Trial, held in September of each year, lasts three days and bring together the 15 best dogs from each National event.

Trials are designed upon the basics of sheep farming (on a hill), and although trials vary slightly from one another, they usually feature the shed, pen, lift, fetch, drive and outrun. Trials are always timed, and the dog is given a certain amount of time to accomplish a series of tasks in conjunction with a handler (shepherd). Amongst the common tasks featured in a sheepdog trial is fetching a few sheep a 200 to

Border Collies love working with sheep farmers...and the feeling is mutual. Sheepdog trials are based on farm work, not on a sleek competitive sport.

Sheepdog trials require that a Border Collie fetch the sheep through a gate, steer them around a handler, drive them away from an obstacle, direct them into a pen, and then run them off the course.

400 yards away and drive them through a series of gates or hurdles. Another task would be singling out a branded or marked animal.

Likely sheepdog trials will grow in popularity and 'outgrow' the farmers. Journalist, shepherd and breeder, Marjorie Quarton laments this possibility: 'A sheepdog trial should be as much a farmer's sport as a ploughing match, not a fancy demonstration in which suitable sheep have to be found to "lead" the dog round the course without any fear of a confrontation.' One thing is certain, regardless of whether sheepdog trials become a public spectacle like agility trials, the farming talents of one single well-bred Border Collie could never be matched, not even by four dozen men on tractors and cycles!

FIELD TRIALS AND WORKING TESTS

Working tests are frequently used to prepare dogs for field trials, the purpose of which is to heighten the instincts and natural abilities of gundogs. Live game is not used in working tests. Unlike field trials, working tests do not count toward

DID YOU KNOW?

You can get information about dog shows from kennel clubs and breed clubs:

Fédération Cynologique Internationale
14, rue Leopold II, B-6530 Thuin, Belgium
www.fci.be

The Kennel Club
1-5 Clarges St., Piccadilly, London W1Y 8AB, UK
www.the-kennel-club.org.uk

American Kennel Club
5580 Centerview Dr., Raleigh, NC 27606-3390, USA
www.akc.org

Canadian Kennel Club
89 Skyway Ave., Suite 100, Etobicoke, Ontario M9W 6R4 Canada
www.ckc.ca

a dog's record at The Kennel Club, though the same judges often oversee working tests. Field trials began in England in 1947 and are only moderately popular amongst dog folk. Whilst breeders of Working and Gundog breeds concern themselves with the field abilities of their dogs, there is considerably less interest in field trials than dog shows. In order for dogs to become full champions, certain breeds must qualify in the field as well. Upon gaining three CCs in the show ring, the dog is designated a Show Champion (Sh Ch). The title Champion (Ch) requires that the dog gain an award at a field trial, be a 'special qualifier' at a field trial or pass a 'special show dog qualifier' judged by a field trial judge on a shooting day.

AGILITY TRIALS
Agility trials began in the United Kingdom in 1977 and have since spread around the world, especially to the United States, where it enjoys strong popularity. The handler directs his dog over an obstacle course that includes jumps (such as those used in the working trials), as well as tyres, the dog walk, weave poles, pipe tunnels, collapsed tunnels, etc. The Kennel Club requires that dogs not be trained for agility until they are 12 months old. This dog sport intends to be great fun for dog and owner and

Training a Border Collie to jump on an obstacle course requires a great deal of equipment, time and patience.

interested owners should join a training club that has obstacles and experienced agility handlers who can introduce you and your dog to the 'ropes' (and tyres, tunnels and so on).

FÉDÉRATION CYNOLOGIQUE INTERNATIONALE
Established in 1911, the Fédération Cynologique Internationale (FCI) represents the 'world kennel club.' This international body brings uniformity to the breeding, judging and showing of purebred dogs. Although the FCI originally included only four European nations: France,

Holland, Austria and Belgium (which remains its headquarters), the organisation today embraces nations on six continents and recognises well over 400 breeds of purebred dog. There are three titles attainable through the FCI: the International Champion, which is the most prestigious; the International Beauty Champion, which is based on aptitude certificates in different countries; and the International Trial Champion, which is based on achievement in obedience trials in different countries.

Quarantine laws in England and Australia prohibit most of their exhibitors from entering FCI shows. The rest of the Continent does participate in these impressive canine spectacles, the largest of which is the World Dog Show, hosted in a different country each year. FCI sponsors both national and international shows. The hosting country determines the judging system and breed standards are always based on the breed's country of origin.

A highly successful junior handler with her award-winning Border Collie. The Kennel Club Junior Organisation welcomes all young people from 8 to 18 years of age. Members participate in competitions, shows, camps and lots more.

UNDERSTANDING THE BEHAVIOUR OF YOUR
Border Collie

As a Border Collie owner, you have selected your dog so that you and your loved ones can have a companion, a protector, a friend and a four-legged family member. You invest time, money and effort to care for and train the family's new charge. Of course, this chosen canine behaves perfectly! Well, perfectly like a dog. When discussing the Border Collie, owners have much to consider. Most behaviourists and trainers regard the Border Collie as the most intelligent dog on the planet. Add to this dog's Einstein-like smarts, its remarkable industry and energy. Owners must be ready to put their thinking caps on when trying to handle the Border Collie.

THINK LIKE A DOG

Dogs do not think like humans, nor do humans think like dogs, though we try. Unfortunately, a dog is incapable of figuring out how humans think, so the responsibility falls on the owner to adopt a proper canine mindset. Dogs cannot rationalise, and dogs exist in the present moment. Many dog owners make the mistake in training of

thinking that they can reprimand their dog for something he did a while ago. Basically, you cannot even reprimand a dog for something he did 20 seconds ago! Either catch him in the act or forget it! It is a waste of your and your dog's time—in his mind, you are reprimanding him for whatever he is doing at that moment.

The following behavioural problems represent some which owners most commonly encounter. Every dog is unique and every situation is unique. No author could purport to solve your Border Collie's problem simply by reading a script. Here we outline some basic 'dogspeak' so that owners' chances of solving behavioural problems are

> **DID YOU KNOW?**
> Punishment is rarely necessary for a misbehaving dog. Dogs that are habitually bad probably had a poor education and they do not know what is expected of them. They need training. Disciplinary behaviour on your part usually does more harm than good.

Training your Border Collie to bring you the newspaper every day is usually simple if the dog has learned the basic commands.

increased. Discuss bad habits with your veterinary surgeon and he/she can recommend a behavioural specialist to consult in appropriate cases. Since behavioural abnormalities are the leading reason owners abandon their pets, we hope that you will make a valiant effort to solve your Border Collie's problem. Patience and understanding are virtues that dwell in every pet-loving household.

AGGRESSION
This is a problem that concerns many dog owners. Although not a big problem in Border Collies, owners should know how to recognise aggressive behaviour. Aggression, when not controlled, always becomes dangerous. An aggressive dog, no matter the size, may lunge at, bite or even attack a person or another dog. Aggressive behaviour is not to be tolerated. It is more than just inappropriate behaviour; it is not safe, especially with a tenacious, powerful breed such as the Border Collie. It is painful for a family to watch their dog become unpredictable in his behaviour to the point where they are afraid of him. Whilst not all aggressive behaviour is dangerous, growling, baring teeth, etc., can be frightening. It is important to ascertain why the dog is acting in this manner. Aggression is a display of dominance, and the dog should not have the dominant role in its pack, which is, in this case, your family.

It is important not to challenge an aggressive dog as this could provoke an attack. Observe your Border Collie's body language. Does he make direct eye contact and stare? Does he try to make himself as large as possible: ears pricked, chest out, tail erect? Height and size signify authority in a dog

DID YOU KNOW?
Physical games like pulling contests, wrestling, jumping and teasing should not be encouraged. Inciting the dog's crazy behaviour tends to confuse a dog. The owner has to be able to control his dog at all times; even in play, your dog has to know you're the leader and you decide when to play and when to behave mannerly.

pack—being taller or 'above' another dog literally means that he is 'above' in the social status. These body signals tell you that your Border Collie thinks he is in charge, a problem that needs to be addressed. An aggressive dog is unpredictable: you never know when he is going to strike and what he is going to do. You cannot understand why a dog that is playful and loving one minute is growling and snapping the next.

The best solution is to consult a behavioural specialist, one who has experience with the Border Collie if possible. Together, perhaps you can pinpoint the cause of your dog's aggression and do something about it. An aggressive dog cannot be trusted, and a dog that cannot be trusted is not safe to have as a family pet. If the pet Border Collie becomes untrustworthy, he cannot be kept in the home with the family. The family must get rid of the dog. In the worst case, the dog must be euthanized.

Border Collies are generally not aggressive dogs, though every individual is different and must be handled as such.

AGGRESSION TOWARD OTHER DOGS

In general, a dog's aggressive behaviour toward another dog stems from not enough exposure to other dogs at an early age. With all dogs, early socialisation with other dogs is absolutely essential. Border Collies are not naturally aggressive toward other dogs, but if other dogs make your Border Collie nervous and agitated, he will lash out as a defensive mechanism. A dog who has not received sufficient exposure to other canines tends to believe that he is the only dog on the planet. The animal becomes so dominant that he does not even show signs that he is fearful or threatened. Without growling or any other physical signal as a warning, he will lunge at and bite the other dog. A way to correct this is to let your Border Collie approach another dog when walking on lead. Watch very closely and at the very first sign of aggression,

> **DID YOU KNOW?**
> Never scream, shout, jump or run about if you want your dog to stay calm. You set the example for your dog's behaviour in most circumstances. Learn from your dog's reaction to your behaviour and act accordingly.

143

correct your Border Collie and pull him away. Scold him for any sign of discomfort, and then praise him when he ignores or tolerates the other dog. Keep this up until he stops the aggressive behaviour, learns to ignore the other dog or accepts other dogs. Praise him lavishly for his correct behaviour.

DOMINANT AGGRESSION

A social hierarchy is firmly established in a wild dog pack. The dog wants to dominate those under him and please those above him. Dogs know that there must be a leader. If you are not the obvious choice for emperor, the dog will assume the throne! These conflicting innate desires are what a dog owner is up against when he sets about training a dog. In training a dog to obey commands, the owner is reinforcing that he is the top dog in the 'pack' and that the dog should, and should want to, serve his superior. Thus, the owner is suppressing the dog's urge to dominate by modifying his behaviour and making him obedient.

An important part of training is taking every opportunity to reinforce that you are the leader. The simple action of making your Border Collie sit to wait for his food says that you control when he eats and that he is dependent on you for food.

Although it may be difficult, do not give in to your dog's wishes every time he whines at you or looks at you with his pleading eyes. It is a constant effort to show the dog that his place in the pack is at the bottom. This is not meant to sound cruel or inhumane. You love your Border Collie and you should treat him with care and affection. You (hopefully) did not get a dog just so you could boss around another creature. Dog training is not about being cruel or feeling important, it is about moulding the dog's behaviour into what is acceptable and teaching him to live by your rules. In theory, it is quite simple: catch him in appropriate behaviour and reward him for it. Add a dog into the equation and it becomes a bit more trying, but as a rule of thumb, positive reinforcement is what works best.

With a dominant dog, punishment and negative reinforcement can have the opposite effect of what you are after. It can make a dog fearful

DID YOU KNOW?
DANGER! If you and your on-lead dog are approached by a larger, running dog that is not restrained, walk away from the dog as quickly as possible. Don't allow your dog to make eye contact with the other dog. You should not make eye contact either. In dog terms, eye contact indicates a challenge.

and/or act out aggressively if he feels he is being challenged. Remember, a dominant dog perceives himself at the top of the social heap and will fight to

Training is moulding your dog's behaviour to suit your desires. Overly dominant dogs may become possessive of your belongings. You certainly don't want your pooch to poach your pillows.

DID YOU KNOW?
Dog aggression is a serious problem. NEVER give an aggressive dog to someone else. The dog will usually be more aggressive in a new situation where his leadership is unchallenged and unquestioned (in his mind).

defend his perceived status. The best way to prevent that is never to give him reason to think that he is in control in the first place. If you are having trouble training your Border Collie and it seems

145

as if he is constantly challenging your authority, seek the help of an obedience trainer or behavioural specialist. A professional will work with both you and your dog to teach you effective techniques to use at home. Beware of trainers who rely on excessively harsh methods; scolding is necessary now and then, but the focus in your training should always be on positive reinforcement.

If you can isolate what brings out the fear reaction, you can help the dog get over it. Supervise your Border Collie's interactions with people and other dogs, and praise the dog when it goes well. If he starts to act aggressively in a situation, correct him and remove him from the situation. Do not let people approach the dog and start petting him without your express permission. That way, you can have the dog sit to accept petting, and praise him when he behaves properly. You are focusing on praise and on

DID YOU KNOW?

Males, whether castrated or not, will mount almost anything: a pillow, your leg or, much to your horror, even your neighbour's leg. As with other types of inappropriate behaviour, the dog must be corrected while in the act, which for once is not difficult. Often he will not let go! While a puppy is experimenting with his very first urges, his owners feel he needs to 'sow his oats' and allow the pup to mount. As the pup grows into a full-size dog, with full-size urges, it becomes a nuisance and an embarrassment. Males always appear as if they are trying to 'save the race,' more determined and stronger than imaginable. While altering the dog at an appropriate age will limit the dog's desire, it usually does not remove it entirely.

modifying his behaviour by rewarding him when he acts appropriately. By being gentle and by supervising his interactions, you are showing him that there is no need to be afraid or defensive.

SEXUAL BEHAVIOUR

Dogs exhibit certain sexual behaviours that may have influenced your choice of male or female when you first purchased your Border Collie. Spaying/neutering will eliminate these behaviours, but if you are purchasing a dog that you wish

DID YOU KNOW?

Your dog inherited the pack-leader mentality. He only knows about pecking order. He instinctively wants to be top dog but you have to convince him that you are boss. There is no such thing as living in a democracy with your dog. You are the dictator, the absolute monarch.

to breed, you should be aware of what you will have to deal with throughout the dog's life.

Female dogs usually have two oestruses per year with each season lasting about three weeks. These are the only times in which a female dog will mate, and she usually will not allow this until the second week of the cycle. If a bitch is not bred during the heat cycle, it is not uncommon for her to experience a false pregnancy, in which her mammary glands swell and she exhibits maternal tendencies toward toys or other objects.

Owners must further recognise that mounting is not merely a sexual expression but also one of dominance. Be consistent and persistent and you will find that you can 'move mounters.'

CHEWING

The national canine pastime is chewing! Every dog loves to sink his 'canines' into a tasty bone, but sometimes that bone is attached to his owner's hand! Dogs need to chew, to massage their gums, to make their new teeth feel better and to exercise their jaws. This is a natural behaviour deeply imbedded in all things canine. Our role as owners is not to stop chewing, but to redirect it to positive, chew-worthy objects. Be an informed owner and purchase proper chew toys like strong nylon bones made for active dogs like your Border Collie. Be sure that the devices are safe and durable, since your dog's safety is at risk. Again, the owner is responsible for ensuring a dog-proof environment. The best answer is prevention: that is, put your shoes, handbags and other tasty objects in their proper places (out of the reach of the

If your Border Collie is a chewer, be sure that you give him chew toys that are strong and safe. Some stuffed toys may contain dyes that might be dangerous.

147

growing canine mouth). Direct puppies to their toys whenever you see them tasting the furniture legs or your trouser leg. Make a loud noise to attract the pup's attention and immediately escort him to his chew toy and

Owners must direct the Border Collie's chewing proclivities toward positive outlets.

engage him with the toy for at least four minutes, praising and encouraging him all the while.

Some trainers recommend deterrents, such as hot pepper or another bitter spice or a product designed for this purpose, to discourage the dog from chewing unwanted objects. This is sometimes reliable, though not as often as the manufacturers of such products claim. Test out the product with your own dog before investing in a case of it.

Some Border Collies are so exuberant with play that they will jump up and frighten guests to your home.

JUMPING UP

Jumping up is a dog's friendly way of saying hello! Some dog owners do not mind when their dog jumps up, which is fine for them. The problem arises when guests come to the house and the dog greets them in the same manner—whether they like it or not! However friendly the greeting may be, chances are

your visitors will not appreciate being knocked over by your boisterous Border Collie. The dog will not be able to distinguish upon whom he can jump and whom he cannot. Therefore, it is probably best to discourage this behaviour entirely.

Pick a command such as 'Off.' (avoid using 'Down' since you will use that for the dog to lie down) and tell him 'Off' when he jumps up. Place him on the ground on all fours and have him sit, praising him the whole time. Always lavish him with praise and petting when he is in the sit position. That way you are still giving him a warm affectionate greeting, because you are as excited to see him as he is to see you!

DIGGING

Digging, which is seen as a destructive behaviour to humans, is actually quite a natural behaviour in dogs. Although your Border Collie is not one of the 'earth dogs' (also known as terriers), his desire to dig can be irrepressible and most frustrating to his owners. When digging occurs in your garden, it is actually a normal behaviour redirected into something the dog can do in his everyday life. In the wild, a dog would be actively seeking food, making his own shelter, etc. He would be using his paws in a purposeful manner for his survival. Since you provide him with food and shelter, he has no need to use his paws for these purposes, and so the energy that he would be using manifests itself in the form of little holes all over your garden and flower beds.

Perhaps your dog is digging as a reaction to boredom—it is somewhat similar to someone eating a whole bag of crisps in front of the TV—because they are there and there is not anything better to do! Basically, the answer is to provide the dog with adequate play and exercise so that his mind and paws are occupied, and so that he feels as if he is doing something useful.

Of course, digging is easiest to control if it is stopped as soon as possible, but it is often hard to catch a dog in the act, especially if he is alone in the garden during the day. If your dog is a compulsive digger and is not easily distracted by other activities, you can designate an area on your property where it is okay for him to dig. If you catch him

DID YOU KNOW?

When a dog bites there is always a good reason for it doing so. Many dogs are trained to protect a person, an area or an object. When that person, area or object is violated, the dog will attack. A dog attacks with its mouth. It has no other means of attack. It never uses teeth for defense. It merely runs away or lays down on the ground when it is in an indefensible situation. Fighting dogs (and there are many breeds which fight) are taught to fight, but they also have a natural instinct to fight. This instinct is normally reserved for other dogs, though unfortunate accidents occur when babies crawl towards a fighting dog and the dog mistakes the crawling child as a potential attacker.

If a dog is a biter for no reason, if it bites the hand that feeds it or if it snaps at members of your family, see your veterinary surgeon or behaviourist immediately to learn how to modify the dog's behaviour.

digging in an off-limits area of the garden, immediately bring him to the approved area and praise him for digging there. Keep a close eye on him so that you can catch him in the act—that is the only way to make him understand what is permitted and what is not. If you bring him

DID YOU KNOW?

If you are approached by an aggressive, growling dog, do not run away. Simply stand still and avoid eye contact. If you have something in your hand (like a handbag), throw it sideways away from your body to distract the dog from making a frontal attack.

to a hole he dug an hour ago and tell him 'No,' he will understand that you are not fond of holes, or dirt, or flowers. If you catch him whilst he is stifle-deep in your tulips, that is when he will get your message.

BARKING

Dogs cannot talk—oh, what they would say if they could! Instead, barking is a dog's way of 'talking.' It can be somewhat frustrating because it is not always easy to tell what a dog means by his bark—is he excited, happy, frightened or angry? Whatever it is that the dog is trying to say, he should not be punished for barking. Only when the barking becomes excessive, and when the excessive barking becomes a bad habit, does the behaviour need to be modified. Fortunately, Border Collies are not as vocal as most other terriers, and they tend to use their barks more purposefully than most dogs. If an intruder came into your home in the

Keeping a Border Collie entertained and active will stimulate his mind and body. Boredom is a common cause of many destructive behaviours.

middle of the night and your Border Collie barked a warning, wouldn't you be pleased? You would probably deem your dog a hero, a wonderful guardian and protector of the home. Most dogs are not as discriminate as the Border Collie. For instance, if a friend drops by unexpectedly and rings the doorbell and is greeted with a sudden sharp bark, you would probably be annoyed at the dog. But in reality, isn't this just the same behaviour? The dog does not know any better...unless he sees who is at the door and it is someone he knows, he will bark as a means of vocalising that his (and your) territory is being threatened. Whilst your friend is not posing a threat, it is all the same to the dog. Barking is his means of letting you know that there is an intrusion, whether

friend or foe, on your property. This type of barking is instinctive and should not be discouraged.

Excessive habitual barking, however, is a problem that should be corrected early on. As your Border Collie grows up, you will be able to tell when his barking is purposeful and when it is for no reason. You will become able to distinguish your dog's different barks and their meanings. For example, the bark when someone comes to the door will be different from the bark when he is excited to see you. It is similar to a person's tone of voice, except that the dog has to rely totally on tone of voice because he does not have the benefit of using words. An incessant barker will be evident at an early age.

There are some things that encourage a dog to bark. For example, if your dog barks non-stop for a few minutes and you give him a treat to quieten him,

he believes that you are rewarding him for barking. He will associate barking with getting a treat, and will keep doing it until he is rewarded.

FOOD STEALING

Is your dog devising ways of stealing food from your cupboard? If so, you must answer the following questions: Is your Border Collie hungry, or is he 'constantly famished' like every other chow hound? Why is there food on the counter top? Face it, some dogs are more food-motivated than others. Some dogs are totally obsessed by a slab of brisket and can only think of their next meal. Food stealing is terrific fun and always yields a great reward— FOOD, glorious food.

The owner's goal, therefore, is to make the 'reward' less

rewarding, even startling! Plant a shaker can (an empty pop can with coins inside) on the counter so that it catches your pooch offguard. There are other devices available that will surprise the dog when he is looking for a mid-afternoon snack. Such remote-control devices, though not the first choice of some trainers, allow the correction to come from the object instead of the owner. These devices are also useful to keep the snacking hound from napping on furniture that is forbidden.

BEGGING
Just like food stealing, begging is a favourite pastime of hungry puppies! It yields that same lovely reward—FOOD! Dogs quickly learn that their owners keep the 'good food' for themselves, and that we humans do not dine on kibble alone. Begging is a conditioned response related to a specific stimulus, time and place. The sounds of the kitchen, cans and bottles opening, crinkling bags, the smell of food in preparation, etc., will excite the chow hound and soon the paws are in the air!

Here is the solution to stopping this behaviour: Never give in to a beggar! You are rewarding the dog for sitting pretty, jumping up, whining and rubbing his nose into you by giving him that glorious reward—food. By ignoring the dog, you will (eventually) force the behaviour into extinction. Note that the behaviour likely gets worse before it disappears, so be sure there are not any 'softies' in the family who will give in to little 'Oliver' every time he whimpers, 'More, please.'

SEPARATION ANXIETY

Your Border Collie may howl, whine or otherwise vocalise his displeasure at your leaving the house and his being left alone. This is a normal case of separation anxiety, and there are things that can be done to eliminate this problem. Your dog needs to learn that he will be fine on his own for a while and that he will not wither away if he is not attended to every minute of the day. In fact, constant attention can lead to separation anxiety in the first place. If you are endlessly coddling and cooing over your dog, he will come to expect this from you all of the time and it will be more traumatic for him when you are not there. Obviously, you enjoy spending time with your dog, and he thrives on your love and attention. However, it should not become a dependent relationship where he is heartbroken without you.

One thing you can do to minimise separation anxiety is to make your entrances and exits as low-key as possible. Do not give your dog a long drawn-out goodbye, and do not lavish him with hugs and kisses when you return. This is giving in to the attention that he craves, and it will only make him miss it more when you are away. Another thing you can try is to give your dog

DID YOU KNOW?
We all love our dogs and our dogs love us. They show their love and affection by licking us. This is not a very sanitary practice as dogs lick and sniff in some unsavory places. Kissing your dog on the mouth is strictly forbidden, as parasites can be transmitted in this manner.

a treat when you leave; this will not only keep him occupied and keep his mind off the fact that you just left, but it will also help him associate your leaving with a pleasant experience.

You may have to accustom your dog to being left alone in intervals, much like when you introduced your pup to his crate. Of course, when your dog starts whimpering as you

DID YOU KNOW?

Dogs left alone for varying lengths of time may often react wildly when you return. Sometimes they run, jump, bite, chew, tear things apart, wet themselves, gobble their food or behave in a very undisciplined manner. Allow them to calm down before greeting them or they will consider your attention as a reward for their antics.

approach the door, your first instinct will be to run to him and comfort him, but do not do it! Really—eventually he will adjust and be just fine if you take it in small steps. His anxiety stems from being placed in an unfamiliar situation; by familiarising him with being alone he will learn that he is okay. That is not to say you should purposely leave your dog home alone, but the dog needs to know that whilst he can depend on you for his care, you do not have to be by his side 24 hours a day.

When the dog is alone in the house, he should be confined to his crate or a designated dog-proof area of the house. This should be the area in which he sleeps and already feels comfortable so he will feel more at ease when he is alone. This is just one of the many examples in which a crate is an invalu-

able tool for you and your dog, and another reinforcement of why your dog should view his crate as a 'happy' place, a place of his own.

COPROPHAGIA

Faeces eating is, to most humans, one of the most disgusting behaviours that their dog could engage in, yet to the dog it is perfectly normal. It is hard for us to understand why a dog would want to eat its own faeces. He could be seeking certain nutrients that are missing from his diet; he could be just plain hungry; or he could be attracted by the pleasing (to a dog) scent. Whilst coprophagia most often refers to the dog eating his own faeces, a dog may eat that of another animal as well

DID YOU KNOW?

The number of dogs who suffer from separation anxiety is on the rise as more and more pet owners find themselves at work all day. New attention is being paid to this problem, which is especially hard to diagnose since it is only evident when the dog is alone. Research is currently being done to help educate dog owners about separation anxiety and about how they can help minimise this problem in their dogs.

if he comes across it. Vets have found that diets with a low digestibility, containing relatively low levels of fibre and high levels of starch, increase coprophagia. Therefore, high-fibre diets may decrease the likelihood of dogs eating faeces. Both the consistency of the stool (how firm it feels in the dog's mouth) and the presence of undigested nutrients increase the likelihood. Dogs often find the stool of cats and horses more palatable than that of other dogs. Once the dog develops diarrhoea from faeces eating, it will likely quit this distasteful habit, since dogs tend to prefer eating harder faeces.

To discourage this behaviour, first make sure that the food you are feeding your dog is nutritionally complete and that he is getting enough food. If changes in his diet do not seem to work, and no medical cause can be found, you will have to modify the behaviour before it becomes a habit through environmental control. There are some tricks you can try, such as adding an unpleasant-tasting substance to the faeces to make them unpalatable or adding something to the dog's food which will make it unpleasant tasting after it passes through the dog. The best way to

The Border Collie will return your good care, responsible ownership and friendship tenfold. You owe it to your canine chum to give him the best you can.

prevent your dog from eating his stool is to make it unavailable—clean up after he eliminates and remove any stool from the garden. If it is not there, he cannot eat it.

Never reprimand the dog for stool eating, as this rarely impresses the dog. Vets recommend distracting the dog whilst he is in the act of stool eating. Another option is to muzzle the dog when he is in the garden to relieve himself; this usually is effective within 30 to 60 days. Coprophagia is seen most frequently in pups 6 to 12 months of age, and usually disappears around the dog's first birthday.

155

My Border Collie

PUT YOUR PUPPY'S FIRST PICTURE HERE

Dog's Name _____

Date _____ Photographer _____